THE SURVIVAL

school
success

Use Your Brain's Built-In Apps to Sharpen Attention, Battle Boredom, and Build Mental Muscle

Ron Shumsky, Susan M. Islascox, and Rob Bell

free spirit
PUBLISHING®

Library of Congress Cataloging-in-Publication Data
Shumsky, Ron.
    The survival guide for school success : use your brain's built-in apps to sharpen attention, battle boredom, and build mental muscle / Ron Shumsky, Susan Islascox, Rob Bell.
        pages cm
    Summary: "Provides ten tools to help students improve executive functions such as focus, motivation, organization, self-monitoring, and more"— Provided by publisher.
    Includes bibliographical references and index.
    ISBN 978-1-57542-482-8 (paperback) — ISBN 1-57542-482-7 () 1. Attention—Study and teaching—Juvenile literature. 2. Listening—Study and teaching—Juvenile literature. 3. Learning, Psychology of—Juvenile literature. 4. Brain—Juvenile literature. 5. Cognition—Juvenile literature. 6. Study skills—Juvenile literature. I. Islascox, Susan. II. Bell, Rob. III. Title.
    LB1065.S537 2014
    370.15'23—dc23   2014015084

The study cited on page 66 is from Lehrer, Jonah. "DON'T!" *New Yorker* 85, no. 14 (May 18, 2009): 26.

Reading Level Grade 5; Interest Level Ages 10–14;
Fountas & Pinnell Guided Reading Level V

Edited by Eric Braun
Cover and interior design by Tasha Kenyon
Illustrations by Lane Raichert and Raichert Media

10 9 8 7 6 5 4 3 2 1
Printed in the United States of America
S18860714

Free Spirit Publishing Inc.
Minneapolis, MN
(612) 338-2068
help4kids@freespirit.com
www.freespirit.com

To all the kids who've taught us what attention is really about.

And to our families for supporting us in writing that up: Hi-chan, Mi-kun, and Naho; Isaac and David; Max and Maya and Christina.

contents

APP 1

YOUR MIND'S SITE SELECTOR

Paying attention when bored to tears

APP 2

YOUR MIND'S PIZZA CUTTER

Slicing work down to size

APP 3

YOUR MIND'S VIDEO SCREEN

Picturing yourself atop Mt. Work

APP 4

YOUR MIND'S CHEERLEADER

Psyching up & getting pumped (for school!)

APP 5

YOUR MIND'S PIGGY BANK

*Choosing work over play
(and what a marshmallow has to do with it)*

attention and success

At a lot of schools, people have this idea that successful students are intelligent, and students who struggle are not. This idea is wrong. There's a lot more to school success than being intelligent, and there's a lot more to school struggles than being . . . *not*.

Take math homework, for example. Maybe you're a math genius, even the greatest genius of all time. That's great, but if you don't do the assignment, you'll get a zero. And doing it requires much more than knowing math. You have to plan ahead and make time. You have to turn off your screens, get to work, stay focused, not space out, work at the right speed, and more.

It takes certain skills to do these things. We call them "attention skills." Others call them "executive functions," "self-directing," or "self-regulation."

1

It doesn't really matter what you call them. What matters is that you use them.

Plenty of evidence shows that attention skills have more influence on school success and life success than intelligence does. That means that if you want to do well in school and beyond (and who doesn't?), controlling your attention is essential.

Even more evidence shows that *not* controlling attention is the number one cause of poor school performance. So if you're doing poorly in school, or if you're just not doing as well as you'd like, it doesn't mean you're not smart. Much more likely is that you're not applying attention well.

Attention Apps

Think of attention this way: It is how you apply yourself and use your intelligence. This book teaches you 10 tools to help you do that. We call them Attention Apps.

> ***Your Brain and Your Mind**
>
> The Apps in this book are for "your mind," the part of you that thinks, imagines, and remembers. All that activity happens in your brain. In this book, we use both words—*mind* and *brain*—to mean the same thing.

Your brain* is like a powerful computer, sort of like a smartphone, but much smarter and more powerful. The Attention Apps enable you to use your brain in ways you might not have known about before or haven't been very good at. With the Apps you can target and solve typical problems—like finishing math projects, staying awake in science class, and taking on work you have little interest in doing.

Better yet, you don't have to buy these Apps. They're already downloaded into your mind, for free. You just have to access them and practice them. This book shows you how.

the payoff: ruling at school—and beyond

Using your Apps greatly increases your chance of doing better at school. Not using them is a gigantic waste.

This table helps show what we mean. Is it worth using your built-in Attention Apps? You make the call.

Use Your Attention Apps	Don't Use Them
Show your intelligence	Feel unintelligent
Get better grades	Get poorer grades
Get adults off your case	Have adults bothering you to • "focus" • "concentrate" • "work harder"
Stay on top of school and schoolwork	Play catch-up, with the clock running out
Make the most of your mind	Waste your mind's potential

Even more, Attention Apps don't just end when school ends. Like it or not, many of the same skills you need in school are also needed in your future. Here's a short list:

- Taking the initiative to do work (rather than putting it off or blowing it off)

- Motivating yourself

- Doing what you have to do, not just what you want to do

- Managing time and meeting deadlines

- Getting along with people

- Learning from mistakes

In short, your Attention Apps will make a big difference today and tomorrow in school. They can also make a big difference 5, 10, 20, and 30 years from now: in your work life, personal life . . . real life.

how to use this book

Every chapter in this book features one Attention App. Each chapter starts with an overview that explains how the App works and what challenge it's used for. After that, you'll find four main sections:

1. **App Operation** shows how to work the App.

2. **App Demonstration** is the story of a student using the App. These are fictional stories based on experiences of real kids we've worked with.

3. **App Practice** provides hands-on activities you can do to learn the App.

4. **What's Your Payoff?** shows what's in it for you. Like the table on page 3, it compares what happens when you use the App to what happens if you don't.

Throughout the book you'll also find:

• **Keeping It Real**—pointers, personal stories, and direct quotes from real students who have used the Apps.

• **Want to Know More?** boxes that explain a little more about the science behind these Apps.

• **Worksheets** to help you practice using the Apps. You can photocopy these or download and print larger versions from www.freespirit.com/school-success.

A **Menu of Attention Apps** is on pages 7–10. The Menu previews all the Apps in the book and helps you get a handle on the skills you'll be mastering. After you've reviewed the Apps in the Menu, we recommend that you start with Your Mind's Site Selector (App 1). That will help you with all the other Apps in the book. Then, refer to the Menu to see which App you want to learn next. If you have a problem right now that you think one of the Apps can help with, feel free to skip ahead to learn that one. Or, if you prefer, start with Apps that seem easier and work your way to harder ones. It's up to you. You'll get the most out of this book if you learn all of the Apps, whatever order you choose.

WHO ARE WE?

We're educators who've been working in schools for a very long time. During that time we've learned something most adults don't know, or at least will never admit. For many kids, school is boring.

Too often, school is about paying attention and working hard when you're seriously checked-out and totally unmotivated. If school were always interesting and engaging, it would be much, much easier to pay attention to— and this book wouldn't be necessary. But often school is *not* (interesting) and so this book *is* (necessary). That's why we wrote it. We want to help kids like you stop feeling stomped on by school and start stomping back.

If you want to tell us about your experience with these Apps, or if you have questions or comments to share, we'd love to hear from you. You can email us at help4kids@freespirit.com or send us a letter at:

Free Spirit Publishing
217 Fifth Avenue North, Suite 200
Minneapolis, MN 55401-1299

List of Reproducible Forms

Larger (8½" x 11") versions of these forms can also be downloaded from www.freespirit.com/school-success as PDFs and printed or used electronically. You can type information directly into the PDFs on your screen.

menu of attention apps

APP 1: YOUR MIND'S SITE SELECTOR

 Just about everyone who's ever been in a classroom has faced this basic problem: How do you pay attention to the teacher when there are much more interesting things to think about? The Site Selector solves this problem. When you use your Site Selector, you click on the "Teacher Site" and turn off other sites. In short, the Site Selector enables you to block out distractions so you can focus.

The next few Apps—Apps 2 through 5—help you with thinking and working hard. In psychology terms, this is called *controlling mental effort*.

Probably, you've been told to "work harder." But, probably no one has actually shown you *how* to do that. The next four Apps make working *hard* a lot *easier*.

APP 2: YOUR MIND'S PIZZA CUTTER

 This App cuts large, intimidating tasks down to size. If you have a lot of homework or a huge project, you "pizza-cut" it into smaller slices. That makes it a lot easier to handle. Pizza-cutting is especially useful when you feel overwhelmed. Sometimes your workload might seem so huge, you just can't bring yourself to start it. But when you cut it down to size, it becomes much more approachable.

APP 3: YOUR MIND'S VIDEO SCREEN

 When facing work that feels hard or pointless, you use Your Mind's Video Screen to *visualize* the benefits of working. These might include getting good grades or overcoming a challenge. In this way, you see reasons to work and goals to strive for.

APP 4: YOUR MIND'S CHEERLEADER

 This App is used for *self-cheering*—giving yourself messages that encourage you to keep trying and to keep going. When not using this App, you're at risk for *self-booing*—giving yourself discouraging messages. When you do that, you're more likely to give up.

APP 5: YOUR MIND'S PIGGY BANK

 This App gets at the basic question of why you do work in the first place. Why should you do something that feels difficult and boring, like staying home and studying for a math test, instead of doing something fun? The reason is because doing schoolwork is saving and investing in your future. When you choose work over fun, you're putting off small rewards now in return for large payoffs later. This is called *delaying gratification,* and Your Mind's Piggy Bank helps you do it.

APP 6: YOUR MIND'S ACTIVATOR

 Have you ever studied for a test and thought you "got it" only to do a lot worse on the test than you expected? Often, the reason is you didn't study actively enough. For many tests, it's not enough to just read over notes or chapters. You have to *do something* with the information. For instance, summarize it in your own words, predict test questions and answer them, and make examples of what you've learned. You use Your Mind's Activator to control how actively you think. When preparing for tests, you crank it up to a level where you can study actively and *really* get it.

APP 7: YOUR MIND'S WORKBENCH

 Your Mental Workbench is a place for holding several things in mind while thinking about something else. It's also called *working memory*—same App, different brand name. To follow instructions, for instance, you need to hold the instructions in mind while thinking about how to do each step. When reading, it's trouble if you forget one paragraph while reading the next. You also have to remember how to spell words while thinking about how to use them in a sentence. You use your Mental Workbench for just about everything at school.

APP 8: YOUR MIND'S SPEEDOMETER

 This App helps you balance speed with accuracy when working. With work that's clear or easy for you, you go full speed ahead. When things get tricky, you slow down and proceed more carefully. Without using Your Mind's Speedometer, you risk working at the wrong speed. You may go too quickly, making careless mistakes in your haste (think 90 mph down a narrow street). Or you may work too slowly, proceeding so carefully that it takes forever (think 20 mph cross country).

APP 9: YOUR MIND'S CALENDAR

So much to do, so little time. For example, if you stay after school for sports practice, you may get home too late to study enough. If you study more, you don't have time to practice your sport and stay in shape. Perhaps you could squeeze in sports and studying, but that wouldn't leave time for friends. What about band, scouts, and tae kwon do? Your Mind's Calendar is used for managing time. It helps you balance what to do with when to do it. Use it for making schedules and sticking to them, planning ahead, and prioritizing.

APP 10: YOUR MIND'S OBSERVER

This App is used for watching yourself. With Your Mind's Observer, you can ask yourself, "How am I doing?" and "How did I do?" Then, if you don't like the answers to those questions, you can change what you're doing. With schoolwork, you use Your Mind's Observer to check your work and see what needs correcting. If you don't use it, you could make the same mistakes again and again.

Your Mind's Observer is even more useful socially. You watch others' reactions to what you say and do, then adjust based on how they react. For example, say you tell a joke and no one laughs. Your Mind's Observer advises you that the joke didn't work and that you ought to give it up. Without this App, you could keep telling the same bad joke over and over, unaware that it's not working.

APP 1
YOUR MIND'S SITE SELECTOR

Paying attention when bored to tears

Picture this . . .

You're sitting in history class. It's 11:30 on Friday, and your stomach is growling because it's almost lunchtime. The weekend is only a couple hours away. And your best friend, who sits right behind you, is telling you about a hilarious YouTube video he saw last night. In front of the class, your teacher is droning on about iron ore production during the Austro-Hungarian Empire.

This poses an all too familiar problem for students. How are you supposed to pay attention to the teacher when there are so many things you'd rather pay attention to? Food, weekend fun, friends . . . pretty much anything other than Austro-Hungarian iron ore.

What's the solution? Use Your Mind's Site Selector to click onto the Teacher Site. Block out the Food Site,

Weekend Site, Best Friend's YouTube Story Site, and everything else that distracts you. That way your attention is
focused where it needs to be: on your teacher.

In other words, controlling attention is kind of like
being online. When you're online, you select one site to
be on and block out the millions of others. With Your
Mind's Site Selector, you do the same thing in class. You
click onto the site you need to pay attention to—your
teacher—and stay off the ones you don't.

It's not your fault if you're easily distracted. Paying
attention to something that's boring to you is just not
natural. To do it requires excellent control of Your Mind's
Site Selector. But you *can* do it, and this chapter shows
you how.

App Operation

Your Mind's Site Selector has several key features for managing attention. Here's how they work:

To start, get a copy of the Site Selector worksheet (see page 28). The electronic version is a PDF you can type into and even add digital pictures to. But you can just write on (or glue pictures to) a paper copy if that's easier. Once you master the Site Selector, you won't need the worksheet anymore.

Think about a class where you have trouble staying focused. Now you're ready to get started.

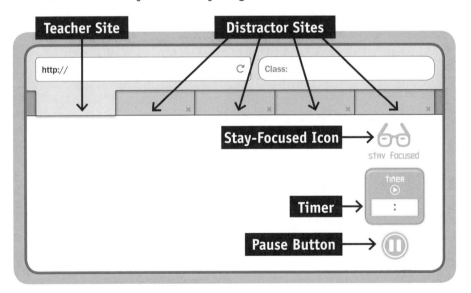

STEP 1.
MAKE THE TEACHER SITE

In the center of the worksheet, under the "Teacher Site" tab, add a symbol of your teacher. This can be a photo, drawing, icon you invent, or simply the name of your teacher. You want this symbol to be bold and

> **⚠ Warning!**
> Offensive and embarrassing teacher pictures can be trouble. Keep it something your teacher won't mind seeing.

noticeable—something you can easily focus on. Use bright colors or decorations, or put a bobbled sombrero on the picture of your teacher. The specifics are up to you. The point is that you want your teacher to stand out, because what stands out is what the mind best pays attention to.

STEP 2.
MAKE THE DISTRACTOR SITES

In the tabs along the top of the worksheet, make symbols for your Distractor Sites. The Distractor Sites are different for everyone. Just make sure your sites are the ones that distract you in class.

Here are a few common ones:

- **Friends Site.** Where your friends distract you

- **Weekend Site** and **Holiday Site.** Where you focus on all the fun times awaiting you outside of class

- **Food Site.** Where you pay attention to feelings of hunger

- **Anxiety Site.** Where you worry, worry, and worry some more

- **Love Site.** Where special feelings for a special someone distract you

- **Imagination & Fantasy Site.** Where you daydream or go off to your happy place

- **Nothing Site.** Where you zone out and think about . . . uh, where were we?

- **Sports Site.** Where baseball, volleyball, skateboarding, snowboarding, or other sports compete for your attention

- **Gaming Site.** Where you obsess over a video game or computer game

- **Hobby Site.** Where a favorite activity like a musical instrument or Lego project distracts you

- **Pet Site.** Where you keep picturing your pet

You can write in your Distractor Sites, as in the picture above. You can also use symbols or icons like these:

What matters is that those sites stay in the tabs and are less interesting than the Teacher Site. That way the Teacher Site stands out as much as possible. When you look at the Site Selector, you want your attention to be drawn to the Teacher Site, not the Distractor Sites.

STEP 3.
SET THE TIMER

The timer helps you keep track of how much longer you have to stay on the Teacher Site. It really helps to be able to see the end. You can focus better because you know that this class will not last forever—even if it seems like it will.

To "set" your timer, determine how long you can realistically focus on the teacher. You do this by thinking about two key factors.

- **The Class.** The first key factor is the class itself, including the teacher. If it's a class that is extremely boring to you, it's probably very hard to pay attention to. That means you should set your timer to just a few minutes. If the class is boring but not *super*-boring, or the teacher is kind of interesting, your tolerance is probably a little higher.

- **The Distractions.** The second key factor is how interesting the Distractor Sites are in that class. Maybe it's the only class all day when you get to see your best friend. That's probably a big distraction. Or maybe the distractions are smaller—for example, gazing out the window at something, anything (or nothing) out there.

Now put the key factors together. If the class is very hard to focus on and the distractions are powerful, you should set your timer for a short amount of time. Five or ten minutes is a good place to start. If your boredom in the class is somewhat tolerable, or the distractions aren't so bad, set your timer for longer. Try 15 or 20 minutes.

Write the number of minutes into the timer space on the Site Selector. Now your timer is set. This is how long you'll pay attention before you hit pause and take a break.

STEP 4.
PLAN YOUR STAY-FOCUSED STRATEGIES

The strategies you use to stay focused are at the heart of your Site Selector App. You'll write them down on your Stay-Focused Strategies planner (found on page 29; you'll need to make or print extra copies). Before you go to class, plan ahead how you'll use each of the strategies on pages 17–20. The planning ahead part is really key. First of all, simply knowing you have a plan can help you stay focused and tuned in. In addition, when your attention starts to drift, you don't have to struggle to figure out what to do. You just follow your plan. (The "Stay-Focused" icon on the Site Selector worksheet will help you remember.)

Strategy: Deal with Distractions

On your Stay-Focused Strategies planner, write the names of your Distractor Sites in the column labeled "Distractor Sites." Then find a way to make each of these Distractor Sites less distracting to you. For example, if you have a distracting friend in the classroom, write "Friend Site" in the Distractor Site column. What can you write in the "My Stay-Focused Strategies" column? One idea is to sit apart from your friend so she can't distract you as easily. Another idea is to talk to her before class and ask her not to bug you so you can concentrate in class. Write at least one way to stay focused for each Distractor Site.

Want to Know More?

Site Selecting helps you direct your own mind. Psychologists call this "selective attention"— selecting what to think about and what to filter out. We call it **putting yourself in charge**. When you're using your Site Selector, you're telling your mind what to think about (for example, the teacher in class) and what not to think about (the distractions). When you're not using your Site Selector, it's almost as if your mind has a mind of its own. It's pulled here, there, and everywhere by this distraction and that distraction, rather than going where you tell it to go.

Strategy: Use Site Selector Language

Just telling yourself to focus and not get distracted rarely works. If your mind is wandering off to the Love Site and you're trying to force it back into algebra, your mind will usually win. Love is probably much more interesting to you than algebra.

So, rather than trying to *fight against* your mind, talk with it. Ask yourself, "What site am I on?" "What site should I be on?" If you're on the wrong site, remind yourself to click back by saying, "It's time to switch sites."

Strategy: Stay Physically Active

Focusing is harder when you have to just sit there and take it. If you move around, it can be easier to focus. But you have to move around in ways that won't get you in trouble.

Stay out of trouble by moving in ways that won't distract others. Twiddling your pencil, bouncing your leg, or subtly stretching at your desk can be very helpful for staying focused and alert. However, tossing your pencil in the air (or sword-fighting with it, or pretending it's a hockey stick, harpoon, or microphone) will get noticed by others—including your teacher. So will stomping your feet on the floor and stretching out loudly. Those are major distractions to you and others in the room.

Just sitting up straight is a simple way to stay active. When we get bored or lose focus, we often start leaning over or slumping. This only makes it harder to stay focused. Remind yourself to sit up straight and lean forward, with eyes on the teacher or the assignment. This will help you stay more alert.

> Keeping It **REAL**
>
> *"I have some breathing exercises I do. I breathe in through my nose and out through my mouth. I take really long breaths, and that takes away my anxiety."*
> *—Ali*

Strategy: Stay Mentally Active

Even more useful than doing something with your body is doing something with your mind:

- **Ask questions.** When you're asking questions in class, you're exercising your mind. You're interacting with the information and the teacher and other students. And you're raising ideas that you want to understand better. All of this helps you stay focused on the Teacher Site.

- **Make connections.** Sure, some parts of school are boring. But when you're making connections to what you're learning, the boredom usually fades away (a little). Making connections means thinking about the subject in ways that go beyond what you're being taught, and—if possible—connecting it to your own life. For example, let's say you're learning about Tweedledum and Tweedledee. Probably boring, but making connections can help: "How are Tweedledum and Tweedledee similar and different?" "Which one do I like more?" "Which one is more like me?" "Do I know anybody who resembles either one?"

- **Take notes.** This is huge. When you're taking notes you're moving, so you're staying physically active. You're also thinking about what's important to write down and thinking about connections in the ideas. All this is way better than just sitting there glazed over and spaced out.

- **Make the teacher stand out.** If your teacher comes into class tomorrow morning wearing a wedding dress, bright orange jumpsuit, or scuba gear, you'll probably click right onto the Teacher Site. Assuming your teacher won't actually wear one of those outfits, you have to use your imagination. Picture your teacher in a wedding dress, scuba suit, or something similarly bizarre, and the Teacher Site should come in much more clearly.

"Talking in class—asking and answering questions—helps me to stay engaged. I didn't do that at first because I guess I'm kind of shy. I also didn't realize how much my teachers like seeing me tuned in. So focusing pays off that way, too."   —Mitch

The Stay-Focused Strategies planner on page 29 has spaces for you to fill in your own details for these strategies. Before going to class, plan ahead by filling in the blanks on the sheet with words or pictures.

STEP 5.
CLICK THE PAUSE BUTTON

When your timer goes off, you've earned a break. A break is a short period when you're not paying attention to the Teacher Site (or whatever else you're working on in class, such as the Group Work Site or Writing Site). In order to make sure your break is short and you can come back from it easily, you need to have a plan.

Timers and Timing

By the way, don't go on break if doing so would be disruptive to others—even if your timer says it's time. If your teacher is talking to you, you're participating in a group activity, or a guest is speaking to class, put off your break until a better time.

First, plan for how long it will be. A good break in class is no more than three minutes. Use your watch, the clock on the wall, or a timer on your phone (in vibrate mode) to make sure you stay on schedule.

Next, plan what you'll do on your break. A good idea is a short visit to one or two of your Distractor Sites. But choose wisely. Visit a site you can actually "click off" and come back from. Don't visit one you're so into that it's really hard to click it off and refocus on the class. If you're really obsessing about your upcoming dance recital, for example, you'd better not go to your Dance Recital Site on break. You can also plan what you'll physically do—stretch, for example. If you're allowed to get up, you can get a drink of water or splash water on your face.

Finally, plan the ending. This is very important because the hardest part of a break is coming back from it. Be sure you know the last thing you'll be doing on break, and stick to it. After you've done that, you know it's time to go back to the Teacher Site.

Use the table on the Stay-Focused Strategies planner to fill in the details of your break.

STEP 6.
DO IT

For the first of couple times you use your Site Selector, bring your worksheet pages with you to class to help you remember your plan. Refer to them when you need a reminder of what to do next. After you've used this App a few times, you'll be able to keep your plan in your head.

App demonstration: ellen

I'm in eighth grade and have problems paying attention in most of my classes except music and art. The worst is health class, which is not only a boring subject for me but also has a very boring teacher, Mr. X. Worst of all, it's first period, so I'm usually still waking up.

I was tired of getting nagged by Mr. X to pay attention and by my mom to raise my grade. So I started using my Site Selector to help me stay focused in this class. Here's what I did.

Ellen

STEP 1.
MAKE THE TEACHER SITE

I drew a picture of Mr. X with bright orange hair sticking out all over on his head. That definitely helps me pay more attention to him.

STEP 2.
MAKE THE DISTRACTOR SITES

I entered my main Distractor Sites for this class. I made these icons smaller and less colorful than the Teacher Site so that they wouldn't stand out as much.

For this class, my main distractions are:

- **Annoyance Site.** I'm constantly thinking how much I dislike this class and how unimportant it seems.

- **Classmates Site.** The kids next to me are always talking. If I ask them to be quiet, they get nasty.

- **Food Site.** I'm usually hungry in this class. It's first period, and often I stay in bed as long as possible in order to delay getting here. So I miss breakfast.

- **Weekend Site.** On Saturday, I'm going to see a movie I've been looking forward to for a long time. Very psyched and really can't wait.

STEP 3.
SET THE TIMER

To determine how long I can realistically stay tuned to the Teacher Site, I looked at the two Key Factors.

- **The Class.** Sadly, I care very little about this subject and I really don't like this class. The teacher often nags me about paying attention, which makes me even less happy to be there.

- **The Distractions.** How much more appealing are the Distractor Sites than the Teacher Site? Infinitely.

With these Key Factors in mind, I realized that I needed to set my timer for a fairly short period of time. I went with 10 minutes.

STEP 4.
PLAN MY STAY-FOCUSED STRATEGIES

Here are the strategies I came up with.

Strategy: Deal with Distractions

I wrote up a plan for each Distractor Site:

- **Annoyance Site.** The best way to reduce my annoyance is to do well in class. If I pay attention and keep up, both Mr. X and my mom are likely to leave me alone, and that will help me feel less annoyed.

- **Classmates Site.** My strategy here is to sit somewhere else in the room, away from the talkers. Then I won't hear them talking.

- **Food Site.** I can't be hungry in class, or I'll never be able to pay attention. So I'll make breakfast the night before—a bagel with cheese and an apple. I'll grab the food when I'm leaving for school and eat it on the way.

- **Weekend Site.** My dad has this lame expression: "A watched pot never boils." Now I know what he means. Just thinking about something and waiting for it to happen only makes it seem like it's taking longer to come. So I'll remind myself that the movie won't come any faster if I keep obsessing about it. If anything, it will feel like it's taking longer. I'll also remind myself that if I keep thinking about the movie instead of the class, I'll be in trouble after the weekend when Mr. X hands out the test.

Strategy: Use Site Selector Language

Site Selector Language means talking with my mind and working with it—rather than forcing it. So, in this class I plan to keep asking myself, "What site am I on now?" and "What site should I be on now?" If my answer to those two questions is not the same, I'll remind myself to "click back on the right site."

Strategy: Stay Physically Active

Mr. X always gives us a five-minute break at the halfway point of class, so that's a built-in chance to be physically active. I'll go to the water fountain during this time. For the rest of class, I made up a stretching and exercising routine that I'll do quietly at my desk so nobody can see it. In this routine, I tighten major muscles (eyes, jaw, shoulders, neck, stomach, legs, toes), then release and relax them.

Strategy: Stay Mentally Active

Here is the plan I made for staying mentally active:

- **Ask questions.** My goal is to ask at least three questions every day in health class. Trying to think of questions helps as much as asking them does.

- **Make connections.** I'll compare each day's lesson to yesterday's to see if I can figure out how Mr. X is building on what we've already learned. I'll also try to figure out how the information might be useful to me. Finally, I'll think of ways I would teach this class if I were the teacher. I bet I could make it way less dull.

- **Take notes.** I got a notebook just for this class.

- **Make the teacher stand out.** Remember how I drew Mr. X with wild orange hair? I'll also *picture* him with big puffy troll hair and imagine it wobbling around as he moves throughout the room. This will help me stay focused and even enjoy myself a little bit.

STEP 5.
CLICK THE PAUSE BUTTON

My timer says I have to pay attention for 10 minutes before taking a break. After 10 minutes, I'm maxed out. My plan for the break today was to go to my Weekend Site for a while and think about the movie I'm going to see. I set a silent timer for three minutes, ensuring I'd get back to the Teacher Site when I saw it go off.

I used another trick today, too. I jotted down what PowerPoint slide we were covering when I went on break.

Then I noted the slide we were on when I tuned back in. This let me see what I had missed and needed to make up. I had planned to double-check with a friend in the class or even ask Mr. X later (though only if I got really desperate).

STEP 6.
DO IT

It felt a little uncomfortable the first time I used the Site Selector in health. I wasn't used to working so hard in there. But the plan works better than just sitting there annoyed and frustrated, so I'll stick with it.

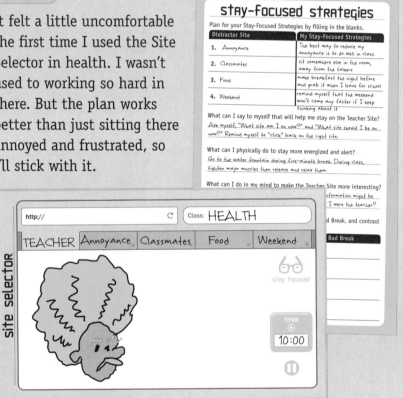

stay-focused strategies

Plan for your Stay-Focused Strategies by filling in the blanks.

Distractor Site	My Stay-Focused Strategies
1. Annoyance	The best way to reduce my annoyance is to do well in class.
2. Classmates	sit somewhere else in the room, away from the talkers
3. Food	make breakfast the night before and grab it when I leave for school
4. Weekend	remind myself that the weekend won't come any faster if I keep thinking about it

What can I say to myself that will help me stay on the Teacher Site?
Ask myself, "What site am I on now?" and "What site should I be on now?" Remind myself to "click" back on the right site.

What can I physically do to stay more energized and alert?
Go to the water fountain during five-minute break. During class, tighten major muscles then release and relax them.

What can I do in my mind to make the Teacher Site more interesting?
...formation might be
...I were the teacher?
...d Break, and contrast

Bad Break

site selector

http://   Class: HEALTH

TEACHER | Annoyance | Classmates | Food | Weekend

stay focused

timer
10:00

app practice

Before you use the Site Selector in class, you'll benefit from a little practice. Here are three exercises you can do to help master your Site Selector before you put it into use at school.

1. PRACTICE STAYING OFF

Think of a class with at least two Distractor Sites. Then come up with at least three ways you can stay off each of those sites.

2. PRACTICE ASKING QUESTIONS

Next time you spend some time with friends or family—for example, at dinner or in the cafeteria—ask at least three questions. If your dad tells a story about his day, what can you ask him about it? If your best friend tells you about a movie she saw, what can you ask her?

3. PRACTICE MAKING CONNECTIONS

While watching a TV show or reading a book, practice connecting what you see or read to other parts of your life. Say a character learns that there's going to be a surprise birthday party for her. The surprise is ruined. What would *you* do in that situation? What do you think she would do if she had *your* friends instead of hers? Would you like it if someone threw you a surprise birthday party? Why or why not? And so on.

what's your payoff?

Use Your Mind's Site Selector	Don't Use It
Stay focused	Get distracted
Pay attention when bored	Pay attention only when interested
Tolerate boredom	Boredom is unbearable
Select what to think about	Think about everything, jump from one thing to another and another in your mind

site selector

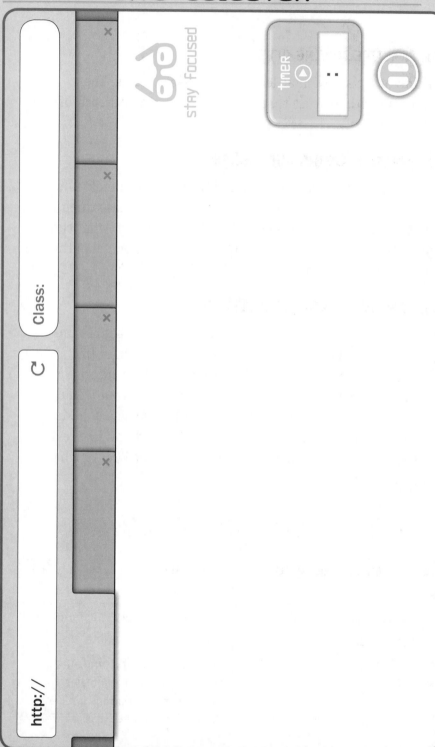

stay-focused strategies

Plan for your Stay-Focused Strategies by filling in the blanks.

Distractor Site	My Stay-Focused Strategies
1.	
2.	
3.	
4.	

What can I say to myself that will help me stay on the Teacher Site?

_____

_____

What can I physically do to stay more energized and alert?

_____

_____

What can I do in my mind to make the Teacher Site more interesting?

_____

_____

In the chart below, fill in the specifics of a Good Break, and contrast that with a Bad Break.

	Good Break	Bad Break
How many minutes?		
What Distractor Sites will I visit in my mind?		
What will I physically do?		
How will I come back to the Teacher Site?		

App 2

Your mind's pizza cutter

Slicing work down to size

Do you procrastinate (put things off until later and later)?
Of course you do—almost everybody does. Does it help you
get your schoolwork done? Of course it doesn't.

Here's a classic example. It's Monday night, and you
have a big project due Friday. But you just can't bring
yourself to get started working on it, so you put it off
until Tuesday. On Tuesday, it still sounds terrible, so you
put it off until Wednesday. On Wednesday . . . well, you
get the idea. Each time you think about that work, it
seems harder and harder to face—and there's less and less
time for finishing it.

Eventually, Thursday night rolls around, and your
options are not good. You can do a last-minute rush job,
pull an all-nighter, or blow it off altogether.

Yes, just about everyone does this. But no, you really don't have to. Your Mind's Pizza Cutter is your procrastination buster. Use your Pizza Cutter to cut down large tasks into manageable pieces. In that way, you make the work much easier to take on.

There are two ways of using Your Mind's Pizza Cutter. Sometimes you have to cut up a Jumbo Pizza. Other times you have to cut up a Combo Pizza.

THE JUMBO PIZZA

Let's say you have to read the novel *The Outsiders* for English class. You have 12 days in which to do it. Coincidentally, the novel has 12 chapters. You could put it off and pretend there's zero English homework for 11 days. Then you'd have to try to read the whole thing in one night.

OR!

You could read one chapter a night and handle this reading assignment fairly easily. One chapter a night is really quite doable. It doesn't seem like a lot of work, so you're much more likely to get to it.

When you take a big, intimidating task and cut it down to size, we call it slicing the Jumbo.

The Outsiders

THE COMBO PIZZA

Sometimes instead of one big task, you have many things to do for different subjects. They might be small things. Maybe none of them alone is very difficult. The problem is the number and variety of jobs. There are so many different tasks that you can get stressed out and frazzled.

This happens in school a lot. Not every assignment involves reading a novel. Often, you have a long list of small jobs from multiple classes: review math facts, write a paragraph for social studies, review notes from STEM class, download this, upload that. The only real difficulties are knowing where to start, figuring out what to do next, and feeling organized and in control.

Pizza-cutting solves the problem. Take that overwhelming list and cut it into individual slices. That makes it easier to see what to do when. With all this in sight, it's much easier to get started.

When you divide up a bunch of smaller tasks into manageable pieces, we call it slicing the combo.

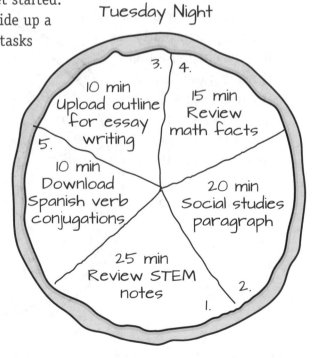

Tuesday Night

3. 10 min Upload outline for essay writing

4. 15 min Review math facts

5. 10 min Download Spanish verb conjugations

20 min Social studies paragraph

25 min Review STEM notes

2.

1.

App Operation

With an actual pizza, you don't just cut wherever you feel like it. There are factors to consider. How big is the pizza? How many people are eating? Are the eaters little kids or adults? The same goes for mental pizza cutting. To best use your Pizza Cutter, consider the following guidelines.

Within these steps you'll also find our Top Four Major Pizza-Cutting Mistakes. Be sure to avoid those!

STEP 1.
ESTIMATE THE TIME YOU'LL NEED

The #1 Major Pizza-Cutting Mistake is underestimating— thinking you can finish work a lot faster than you actually can. Be realistic when estimating time. Look at how long you really need to spend on your work rather than how long you'd *like* it to take. Also, play it safe. If you're not sure whether a project will take two hours or three, choose three.

> Keeping It
> **REAL**
>
> *"Sometimes it takes me a little bit more time than I expected to finish. You have to be flexible with your time. It depends on the work. If it's an essay, it sometimes takes me longer because I have to proofread it and everything. For my next essay, I know I have to plan for more time."* —Mimi

STEP 2.
ESTIMATE ALL YOUR SCHOOLWORK

Be sure to look at *all* your assignments before slicing. Forgetting that is Major Pizza-Cutting Mistake #2. For example, you cut all your science homework into perfect slices . . . but totally ignore social studies and math.

STEP 3.
STAY ON TOP OF OTHER RESPONSIBILITIES

If you are like 99.9 percent of students, you have things other than schoolwork you also need to do. Overlooking these other responsibilities is Major Pizza-Cutting Mistake #3.

For example, you have two hours of homework and decide to do it between 8 and 10 in the evening. That would be fine if you didn't also have to walk the dog and practice trombone during the same time.

STEP 4.
ESTIMATE HOW MUCH ENERGY YOU HAVE—AND WHEN

Look at how you feel on each day and give yourself more work on the days when you can handle it. For example, say you usually come home early and energetic on Tuesdays, but late and tired on Wednesdays. In that case, you should slice off bigger pieces of homework on Tuesdays.

STEP 5.
START WITH HARDER WORK

Look at all your slices and take on the harder ones first. That way, you do the hard work when feeling freshest. You do the easier work later, when you're likely to be tired, because it doesn't require as much mental energy.

Too often, people do this backward, starting with the easy stuff first because it's

Top Four Major Pizza-Cutting Mistakes
Avoid these pitfalls at all costs!

1. Underestimating the time you'll need.
2. Underestimating (or forgetting about) other schoolwork you need to do.
3. Underestimating (or forgetting about) other responsibilities you have (like chores).
4. Doing the easy work first.

easy. And when they do, they end up facing the harder work later, when they have less energy and motivation. This is Major Pizza-Cutting Mistake #4.

STEP 6.
PRIORITIZE

Figure out what absolutely, positively has to be done now and what can wait. If you have math due tomorrow but have to read *The Outsiders* over the next 12 days, you need to make sure you do your math tonight. You should read a chapter of *The Outsiders* if you have time. But if you have to choose, math wins.

App Demonstration: Diego

I'm a sixth grader, and right now, I'm swamped at school. Too much work, not enough time. You've never felt that way, right? Well, I decided to use my mind's Pizza Cutter to slice up all of my work into pieces; that way I'm not over-loaded. Here's an example.

SLICING THE JUMBO

In science class last Monday, Ms. Y told us that we would have a test on Friday. For the test we had to memorize the 40 most common plant forms in our local environment.

My first thought was: "Too much, too hard." And even though I usually like science, memorization is boring. Every time I opened my science book, all I wanted to do was close it again—and open YouTube. Seriously, I didn't even want to get started. But I knew that if I didn't make a plan on Monday to do pieces of my work every night, it would leave me with a huge cram session on Thursday

Diego

night. And that *never* goes well for me. With my Pizza Cutter, I divided the task into smaller parts.

Step 1. Estimate the time I'd need. At first I thought memorizing the plant forms would take only an hour. But then I realized I was underestimating. That wouldn't have given me time to review everything thoroughly. Realistically, this was going to take me about three hours.

Step 2. Estimate my other schoolwork. I had a big math test on Tuesday morning, so I knew I'd want to spend Monday night studying for that. That would mean a little less time for science that night.

Step 3. Stay on top of other responsibilities. It was a busy week. I had tennis practice and a saxophone lesson on Wednesday. Thursday right after school I had a dentist appointment. I knew I'd need to plan around those things.

Step 4. Estimate the energy I would have, and when. I knew that I would have high energy on Tuesday. My math test would be over and I wouldn't have anything going on later. With tennis and sax after school on Wednesday, I knew I'd be tired that evening.

Step 5. Start with harder work. I already knew some of the plant forms on the list because we'd gone over them in class. So I planned to study those last.

Step 6. Prioritize. Math was my priority Monday night, to get ready for Tuesday's test. Wednesday, with tennis and saxophone after school, my top priority in the evening was to relax. That left plant forms as high priority for Tuesday and Thursday.

Now I was ready to slice:

- **Monday.** I had the math test the next morning, so I planned to review plants for only 20–30 minutes and spend an hour studying math.

- **Tuesday.** I would get home early with no other work to do. I planned to study before dinner when not tired and a little more after dinner when I would have less energy (about 90 minutes total).

- **Wednesday.** I would be tired after tennis and sax. I also had to do the dishes and walk the dog, so I planned to study only 20–30 minutes.

- **Thursday.** My entire evening was free, although I figured my mouth was going to be sore after the dentist. I planned to study 45 minutes to an hour.

App Practice

The best way to practice Your Mind's Pizza Cutter is to start using it for your schoolwork. When you start out, use the handout on page 40.

1. Write all the tasks you have to do in the blank space above the empty pizza.

2. Using your pencil as a pizza cutter, cut the multiple tasks into individual slices. Include when you plan to accomplish each slice and how long you'll work on it. Match slice size to time required: larger slices equal longer time. Use the example below for a model.

Diego's Jumbo Pizza:
Study for Friday's Science Test

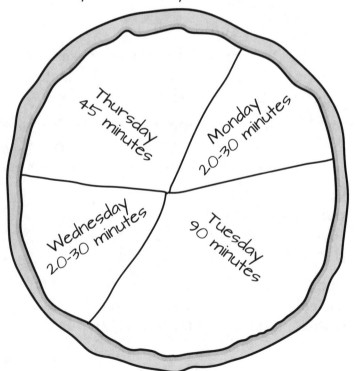

whAt's youR pAyoff?

Use Your Mind's Pizza Cutter	Don't Use It
Cut hard work down to size	Hard work stays intimidating
Feel organized and together when you have many things to do	Feel disorganized and scattered
Make work approachable and take-on-able	Procrastinate—put off work until later, then later, then later . . .
Get to work, feel relief from getting it done, move on to what you enjoy doing	Avoid work, with that lingering and nagging feeling that you should be doing it
Get better results from staying on top of your work and getting to it	Get lousy results from doing last-minute rush jobs

your mind's pizza cutter

Combo Pizza   **Jumbo Pizza**

(circle one)

_____

_____

_____

_____

Divide your pizza into slices. Label each slice with a task that needs to be done, along with the amount of time it will take. Along the outside of the crust, prioritize your slices (first, second, third, etc.).

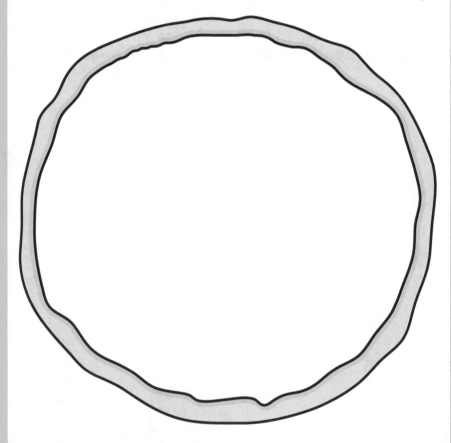

APP 3
your mind's video screen

Picturing yourself atop Mt. Work

You're staring at a mountain of homework. It looks really hard. It feels really dull, like it has nothing to do with your life. Basically, you're not seeing any reason to do it.

Your Mind's Video Screen to the rescue! This App helps you picture the benefits and upsides of working—the reasons to work. Other names for this are *positive imagery* or *positive visualization*.

Dear Ron, Susan, and Rob,

I have a friend who puts zero mental effort into academics but works very hard on baseball and swimming. He gets up before dawn to swim, and he runs for miles in rain and snow. He goes to the batting cages four times a week. Yet he gives up after 10 minutes of science homework. Can you explain this?

Sincerely,
Wondering in Wyoming

Dear Wondering,

The explanation is *imagery*. Your friend pictures vivid and exciting mental images about succeeding as an athlete. These images might involve scenes like making a game-winning catch, hitting a home run, and winning a swim meet. The problem is that he is not creating the same images when studying. While the benefits of practicing sports are clear to him, the benefits of schoolwork are not. Worse yet, he may actually see negative images about schoolwork—failing and being called a loser. With those negative outcomes on his mind's Video Screen, there's little reason to invest effort.

Sincerely,
Ron, Susan, and Rob

App OpeRAtion

Follow these quick and fairly easy steps to good visualizing.

STEP 1.
FIND BENEFITS

In order to visualize the benefits of working hard, you first have to identify those benefits. Here are a few popular examples:

- Something enjoyable when you finish work: game time, snack, music, down time

- A feeling of accomplishment from meeting and beating the challenge, like conquering a mountain of work

- Something enjoyable or interesting within the work: sometimes even the dullest schoolwork has parts that are somewhat interesting

- Adults getting off your case, less checking up on you

- Short-term benefits: good grades, approving teacher, proud parents

- Long-term benefits: getting into college, learning something that enriches your life

Feel free to use one of these, or make up your own. What's important is that you select at least one benefit— one good reason to do the assignment at hand.

Keeping It REAL

"The satisfaction I love is when I don't understand something and then I take the time to understand it and I get it. Like last year in science we learned about blood groups and stuff, but it didn't make sense. So I just took the time to understand it, and, yeah—it was satisfying. That's my reward." —Hailey

"Hailey's thing about finding satisfaction in learning doesn't work for me at all. My attitude is pretty much, 'Why do we need to know this?' But I love getting A's, so when I'm working on some useless assignment about whatever, I picture what the A will look like when I get it back, what color it will be, its shape and size, where it'll be on the page, how great I'll feel when I see it, my parents' reaction when I show it to them." —Vlad

STEP 2.
DRAW OR WRITE THE BENEFIT YOU CHOOSE

Draw a picture of the benefit you choose, or get a photo of it if appropriate. Drawing stick figures is fine. If you prefer, you can write down the benefit.

STEP 3.
VISUALIZE THE BENEFIT

Images will motivate you when, and only when, you can really picture them. It's usually better to visualize with your eyes closed, especially when you're just learning to visualize. That way you can focus on what you see in your mind rather than what's around you. To make your pictures vivid and meaningful, include as many details as possible. Use the acronym CAFE to help guide you. CAFE stands for color, action, feeling, and exaggeration.

- **Color.** For most people, images come to mind more clearly when pictured in color than in black and white. So, what colors are in your image?

- **Action.** Images are stronger when they include action. What do you see happening in your image?

- **Feeling.** What emotions are you feeling in the image? What expressions are you making? Feelings can be stronger when you combine your visual image with other senses. What do you hear, feel, smell, or taste?

- **Exaggeration.** Images are stronger when they stand out from the ordinary. You're much more likely to remember your ride to school tomorrow if you see an elephant on the road. So picture something exaggerated and unusual about your image.

App demonstration: Alfonzo

Basketball is my life. Since I was 10 years old, all I've really wanted to do is play big-time college ball. So when I look at homework, I keep my eyes on the prize.

Take last night's geometry assignment from Ms. Z: "Do exercises 1–18, finding the area and hypotenuse of these

Alfonzo

isosceles triangles." I don't particularly care about isosceles triangles or hypotenuses, and you probably don't either. But I know that doing this assignment gets me a step closer to where I want to go. Here's how I used my mind's Video Screen to get through it.

STEP 1.
FIND BENEFITS

There are a few benefits I could go with here. I could promise myself a chocolate bar after I'm done, or I could focus on how proud my dad will be if I do well in this class. But those aren't going to motivate me as much as the one big reason I have for doing this assignment. That reason is this: When I do well in school, it makes me look better to college recruiters. Every time I nail an assignment, it's another step toward a college basketball scholarship.

STEP 2.
DRAW OR WRITE THE BENEFIT I CHOOSE

Here's me in my college basketball uniform at the University of Michigan.

STEP 3.
VISUALIZE THE BENEFIT

Here are the details of the image I picture when I close my eyes.

- **Color.** I'm on the court at the University of Michigan. A giant *M* at center court is dark blue, and the rest of the court is yellow. My uniform is a shiny gold. The stands are filled with fans wearing gold and blue.

- **Action.** I see myself hitting the game-winning shot against Ohio State at the buzzer.

- **Feeling.** I hear the swish of the ball going through the net and the squeaks of sneakers on the court. I hear the crowd roaring. I smell the leather of the ball and the popcorn in the concession stands. I feel the ball's grip. What I feel is "awesomeness."

- **Exaggeration.** After the game, the Celtics come over and offer me a multimillion-dollar contract.

Oh, yeah, that will do it. As I worked through those 18 geometry proofs, I closed my eyes and visualized that scene every time I noticed my attention start to fade. Before I knew it, I was done.

App Practice

Visualization can be tricky at first. Not everyone feels natural picturing detailed, positive images in their mind. It helps to practice a few times when you are not under too much pressure. So, for the first couple of times, choose an assignment that is not too big or that you aren't too worried about.

For your practice and for the real thing, you can use the worksheet on page 49. Make a copy of the page or download an electronic form.

1. On the lines at the top of the page, write in your hard work or challenging task.

2. In the video screen below the lines, draw or write the benefits you choose—what you will visualize to help motivate you to tackle the challenge. Remember to include lots of details.

3. Close your eyes and picture what's on the screen. To make your picture come to life, include CAFE: Color, Action, Feeling, and Exaggeration.

Your goal is to eventually not need this worksheet and create pictures inside your own mind. So start by using this form, then put it away it once you're creating vivid images in your mind without it.

What's your payoff?

Use Your Mind's Video Screen	Don't Use It
When looking at hard work, see the benefits of doing it	When looking at hard work, see only hard work
Feel motivated by the benefits you see	Don't feel motivated
See goals to strive for	See no point to doing this stuff
See yourself victorious, conquering the hard work and reaching the mountaintop	Stay at the bottom of the mountain looking up

USING YOUR MIND'S VIDEO SCREEN

WHAT IS THE CHALLENGE OR HARD WORK YOU NEED TO ACCOMPLISH?

_____

_____

_____

In the video screen below, draw or describe in writing the benefit to doing this work.

APP 4

YOUR MIND'S CHEERLEADER

Psyching up & getting pumped (for school!)

When taking on hard work, it's important to give yourself encouraging messages—to pump yourself up and cheer yourself on. In other words, to *self-cheer*. The fancy term for this is *positive self-talk*. There's a lot of evidence that doing it can be very motivating. In this chapter, we show you how to talk to yourself positively. You'll also get to practice taking negative messages and turning them into positive ones.

Self-cheering has two main parts. The first is the words you use. Talking is not just something you do out loud with other people. It's also something you do with yourself in your own mind. And what you say to yourself can either *encourage* mental effort or *discourage* it. Telling yourself, "I can't do this, I'll never get it done" is discouraging. You get a very different message when you tell yourself, "I'll feel great when I finish."

The second part of cheering is the emotion you feel. Your feelings can have a powerful effect on your mental effort. For instance, go to a high school football game and listen to the words in the cheers. They're usually something like this:

WE'RE GOING TO THE TOP.
WE'RE NEVER GONNA STOP.
GO, GO, GO!

HEY, HEY.
TODAY IS THE DAY
WE BLOW YOU AWAY!
HOORAY!

HERE WE GO MUSTANGS, HERE WE GO!

The words aren't so inspiring, but that doesn't matter. What matters is that all these cheers have the F WORD. Yes, the cheers generate Feeling, and it's the feeling that drives effort. In fact, many cheers have no words at all. It's the roar of the crowd that gets adrenaline flowing and confidence pumping.

Staying with high school football, check out the pregame when the players race onto the field. They're jumping all around and bashing into each other. These players are psyched and pumped. They're ready to devote every ounce of their effort to the game.

Of course, self-cheering doesn't just apply on the football field. It's the same in the classroom, the science lab, and the library. To work hard in school, you need to create the roar of the crowd in your own mind. You need to psyche yourself up like a middle linebacker to take on schoolwork with the feeling that you're going to nail it.

I AM TOTALLY GONNA ROCK THIS SPANISH VOCAB!

Want to Know More?
Visualization (like in App 3) and self-talk are widely used by counselors, especially for anxiety and depression. That's because there's a lot of evidence that the images we picture in our minds, and the messages we tell ourselves, have a huge impact on how we feel. Constantly picturing failure and putting ourselves down can lead to feeling anxious or depressed. But learning to visualize and self-talk more positively can really turn that around.

Many students don't self-cheer enough. Many are *self-booing* instead. And just like self-cheering, self-booing involves both words and feelings.

Self-booing word messages may be "This work is totally pointless, why bother" or "I'll mess up, so why even try." Feeling messages are often more powerful and might include feeling stupid or feeling like you suck. Other feeling messages are directed outward. For example, you might feel like the work itself is stupid or school sucks. But often these are covers for feelings about oneself.

App Operation

To start using Your Mind's Cheerleader, start with simple cheers and work your way to cheers that have more feeling.

STEP 1.
WRITE SELF-CHEERS

Write out cheers, or think them in your mind. Say these cheers to yourself to help you feel confident about work. Here are some cheerleading tips:

- Focus the cheers on positive statements: "I can pass this test" is better than "I'm not going to fail."

- Emphasize your role using "I" statements: "I can figure this out" is better than "It'll turn out okay."

- Have some belief in the positive statement—don't just do the exercise because this book told you to. It helps to keep the cheer realistic. For example, don't cheer, "I will get 100 percent on this week's test" when you can't be sure of that. Instead, cheer, "I have studied a lot and I will do fine" or "I will focus and work hard."

- Time your cheers for when you need a lift, before you're totally down and out. At a football game, cheerleaders jump in before a key play, or when energy is starting to run low. Cheering has little value once it's game over.

Keeping It **REAL**

"In my mind I tell myself, 'Okay, you've got this. You can do it.' Silly words of encouragement are actually the best for me. I recommend it."   **—Ali**

STEP 2.
TURN AROUND SELF-BOOS

Everyone self-boos sometimes, and no one self-cheers all the time. However, if you're self-booing much more than self-cheering, it can get in the way of working hard. In that case, start by identifying common self-boos and changing them into self-cheers. You can start by making a table like the one below with two columns. Put your self-boos in the left column. In the right column, replace them with self-cheers.

Self-Boos	Self-Cheers
I'm no good at writing.	Writing isn't my thing, but I'm good at other things.
I can't do this project.	If I focus and stay focused, I can finish.
I'm going to fail.	I've studied a lot. Whenever I study this much, I always pass.
I can't stand this assignment	I like the challenge of finishing work I can't stand.

STEP 3.
BREAK THE NEGATIVE CYCLE

Your mental effort increases when your mind and heart work together—when thinking works together with feeling. The hardest part of cheerleading is encouraging yourself when you're feeling down and not succeeding. What can you say to yourself if you're messing up in school—if you're getting D's and F's while your friends and siblings get A's and B's?

First of all, D's and F's usually come gradually. Let's say you get a C on a math test and self-boo, "I'm lousy at math." As a result, you study very little for the next test because you believe you're bad at it and won't do well. This leads to a C-, and that leads to you thinking, "I'm really terrible at math." For the following test, you feel even more discouraged and study even less. You get a D and do more self-booing. By the final, your self-booing has gotten so bad you think you're hopeless and stupid. You blow off studying altogether and get an F.

It's like striking out in baseball and then whacking yourself on the knee in frustration. Next time at bat, your knee is so sore that you strike out again, which you deal with by smashing yourself in the foot. Eventually, you've beaten yourself up so much you have no chance of getting a hit.

So catch yourself before whacking your knee. Rather than studying less after a C or putting yourself down, address the problem. Check with your teacher to fix what you did wrong. Then study differently next time— take extra batting practice. That way, you will break the self-booing cycle.

By the way, doing something badly doesn't make you bad. Maybe math really is extra-hard for you. So what? That doesn't mean you're stupid, and it doesn't mean you're a bad person. Almost everybody struggles with something. What it does mean is that you have trouble learning math and that you'll need extra effort and extra

> **Keeping It REAL**
>
> *"'Just suck it up and do it' is what I tell myself to get working. If I have a hard time with one class, I can just suck it up and do it because I remember that it's not like I can't do anything. I can do the work for the other classes; it's just the one class that's bad."*
>
> *—Thomas*

time to get it. That's a very different message from "I'm bad" or "I'm stupid," and is much more motivating.

STEP 4.
FIND YOUR FIGHT SONG

Watch the movie *Rocky*, the first one. There's a scene where Rocky is training to fight the undefeatable champion. He's racing triumphantly up the Philadelphia Museum of Art steps in the dead of winter with the *Rocky* theme song in the background. It may seem corny and dated, but its appeal is hard to deny. (*Rocky* even won the Academy Award for Best Movie.) You can't help but get swept up by the music and believe that you, too, can succeed against all odds.

For school, find your own *Rocky* theme song. There will always be times you have to push yourself to the max or beyond. At those times, a song can psych you up on a level that words alone just can't reach.

Perhaps you already have a favorite fight song. Many people do. But do you use it for schoolwork? Probably not. *Should* you use it for schoolwork? Definitely. If music helps you feel pumped up for physical and personal challenges, it can work for mental challenges, too.

So the next time you have to study something really hard, listen to your fight song or play it in your mind. It also works to make a playlist of fight songs that fire you up.

Keeping It REAL

"The music that I need depends on the task I have to do. For some work, I need slow, calm music to get me in the mood. When I have to do work that doesn't take a lot of thinking, I like to listen to electro music."
—**Kenta**

Check out our favorites:

Top 10 Psych-Up Classics
1. "Gonna Fly Now" (theme from *Rocky*) by Bill Conti
2. "Eye of the Tiger" by Survivor
3. "It's My Life" by Bon Jovi
4. "Not Giving In" by Rudimental
5. "How Far We've Come" by Matchbox Twenty
6. "We Are the Champions" by Queen
7. "We Will Rock You" by Queen
8. "My Way" by Frank Sinatra
9. "Firework" by Katy Perry
10. "For Those About to Rock (We Salute You)" by AC/DC

App demonstration: Sonia

I had this huge, and I mean *huuuuge*, project to do on the geography of North America. I put it off because I hated the whole idea. It seemed hard and like way too much work. Did I mention it was huge? And I couldn't think of any time in my life I would need to know about land forms.

Still, I knew I had to do it. So I used my mind's Cheerleader to change how I felt about the assignment. Here's what I did.

STEPS 1 AND 2.
WRITE SELF-CHEERS AND TURN AROUND SELF-BOOS

The first thing I had to do was put a stop to all the bad messages I was telling myself. You can see my old self-booing thoughts on the left side of the table below. On the right side of the table you can see how I changed them into self-cheers.

Self-Boos	Self-Cheers
This is totally pointless. When will I ever use this in real life?	Once I get this done, I'll never have to deal with it again.
This report will turn out lousy, just like the last one.	I know what I did wrong last time, so now I know what to fix.
This is unbelievably boring.	That's what I always say, but once I get into it, I usually find something interesting.

I repeated these self-cheers to myself whenever I noticed one of the self-boos creeping in. Sometimes I even said them out loud. I know, embarrassing! But nobody was around to hear me, and it really helped keep me feeling positive while I worked on my report.

STEP 3.
BREAK THE NEGATIVE CYCLE

Earlier this year I wrote a book report, and I didn't do very well on it. But I talked to my teacher afterward, and she gave me some tips on making an outline ahead of time. She also helped me see how to write a strong conclusion. When I started to feel hopeless about this paper on North American geography, I reminded myself that I've learned a lot since I got that low grade last semester. I thought about the hard work I've put in. That helped me break the negative cycle.

STEP 4.
FIND MY FIGHT SONG

For even more help, I put on my fight song before I started working. It's this song called "We Are the Champions" by Queen. It's a really old song, but it makes me feel psyched up because the singer talks about how he keeps on fighting no matter what. I like the idea that he doesn't give up. Neither will I! Sometimes I'll take a break from working and replay the song again.

Sonia

I turned in the paper on time, and I actually feel proud of it. I haven't gotten my grade back yet, but I'm not too nervous. I know I put a lot of work into it, and it will be fine.

App Practice

To get the hang of Your Mind's Cheerleader, practice all the different parts. Start by choosing an assignment, test, or job you have to do. Then follow these instructions.

1. WRITE SELF-CHEERS

Write at least three self-cheers about the task. Remember the ground rules from page 53:

- Make them positive.
- Focus on the "I."

- Believe in them (and make them believable).
- Use them before you are too far down.

2. TURN AROUND SELF-BOOS

Make a two-column list. Title the left column "Self-Boos" and the right column "Self-Cheers." Under "Self-Boos," fill in statements you commonly say to yourself that discourage working hard. Under "Self-Cheers," transform those into self-encouraging statements.

Self-Boos	Self-Cheers
I can't, I can't, I can't.	I will, I will, I will.

3. BREAK THE NEGATIVE CYCLE

Problems and setbacks are a normal part of life. Everyone strikes out sometimes. That's okay. What matters is how you deal with it and how you respond. So practice that here. In the first column, put in problems you've had. In the second column, list responses that make the problems

Problem	Putdown that makes problem larger	Solution that will actually help
Strike out	Break the bat over your knee	Fix your swing
Get a C- on your social studies test	Blame the teacher; give up, quit studying	Get extra help; learn study strategies

worse. In the third column, add what you can do to make things better.

4. FIND YOUR FIGHT SONG

List up to 10 songs that pump you up and make you feel energized. If you don't have any already, take a few days to listen to songs you already know, as well as new songs on the radio or online. You may find some psych-up ideas. You can also ask your friends and family what songs get them fired up.

what's your payoff?

Use Your Mind's Cheerleader	Don't Use It
Tell yourself messages that encourage working hard	Tell yourself discouraging messages
Believe in yourself; feel yourself taking on the challenge and beating it	Believe you're going to strike out and fail
Remind yourself that you have value, even when you mess up or do badly	Feel like you are bad
When the going gets tough, keep trying	Give up when things get difficult
Handle setbacks; fix problems	Respond to setbacks and problems by putting yourself down (which leads to more setbacks and problems)

APP 5

your mind's piggy bank

Choosing work over play (and what a marshmallow has to do with it)

Your Mind's Piggy Bank is used to *delay gratification.* That's a slightly difficult term for a very important skill. Delaying gratification involves putting off small rewards now in return for bigger and better rewards later.

You face this choice all the time. For example, should you watch TV or do your homework? Watching TV would be fun and relaxing right now. But doing your homework will give you a reward later. It's like saving in a bank. When you save money rather than spend it, it starts to add up. As time goes by, you will have lots more money to use later on.

This is what school is all about: Studying and hard work now lead to benefits later. Good grades lead to a good report card, which can lead to a good college, which can lead to a better job. All that can lead to a happier, more comfortable life. Studying now also gives you knowledge and skills that you might not notice or care about today but can help a lot later. If you can delay gratification, you have a huge skill for school success—and future success, too.

Look at these pictures. In the first picture, a student chooses immediate gratification. He has pushed his books aside in favor of playing video games. In the picture on the right, you see what happens later. He gets a lousy report card, and his dad takes away his video game for a month.

In contrast, the girl in the pictures below has decided to delay gratification. There's a game she loves to play on her smartphone, but she keeps the phone turned off and

put away until she completes her homework. In the second picture, delaying that gratification has led to a much bigger reward than fun on a game: She has graduated from college and has a bright future ahead.

By the way, delaying gratification does not mean you never choose to have fun. It only means that you have the patience and mental muscle to put off fun until your work is done.

App Operation

To understand how Your Mind's Piggy Bank works, you need to know about a few important concepts.

KEY PIGGY BANKING CONCEPTS

Present You vs. Future You

When choosing whether to delay gratification, you're often choosing between what's good now and what's good later. When you select good now—for example, checking out Instagram instead of reading your science textbook— you're putting Present You ahead of Future You.

So, why do something difficult or annoying (schoolwork) rather than something you actually enjoy? Because schoolwork is an investment in your future. It's a way of being kind to your future self, not just your present one. And maybe you already know that. But it's not always easy to keep this in mind when social media or video games are calling your name. At those times, it can help to have an image of Future You in mind. Picture what you want your life to look like in the future, and remember that image when you feel tempted to blow off work.

Seeing Progress Is Part of the Payoff

Even if you do think about Future You, it can be hard to stay motivated when your goals seem too far in the future. The payoff feels too distant. Why do something you really don't feel like doing tonight—just because you'll be better off 20 years from now?

To help motivate yourself, build in closer goals along the way. When saving up to buy new headphones, for example, it's very rewarding to see your savings add up and the purchase draw near. The same applies for school. You reach large, distant goals like college and a good job by meeting many smaller goals along the way. A good grade at the end of the semester comes from doing well on tests each month. And doing well on tests comes from studying for quizzes each week and doing homework each night. Every time you turn in an assignment on time or get a good result on a test, imagine that it's a coin dropping into a jar or piggy bank. Every little bit brings you closer to your goal.

"Our Spanish teacher asked each of us to pick a goal to work on for a semester. We each decorated our own plastic container and wrote our goal on the lid. I decided to learn five new vocabulary words each class period. Each day, we would put one piece of candy into our container if we reached our goal. Some of us got into it right away and the candy started to build up. Others weren't serious about it at first. Later, they started feeling left out and began to really work on their goals. By the end of the semester, studying vocab became part of my routine. I knew many more Spanish words, and I had a bunch of candy."

— Daphne

Hard Work Has Value

Strange as it may sound, working hard has a lot of positives. It can feel good when you're really applying yourself. It can feel even better when you take on something you think you can't do and find that you *can* do it by sticking with it. That's a feeling you can take to the next challenge and the challenge after that.

And sure, working hard isn't always "fun." But fun can be a lot more fun when you work first and play second (when you "delay gratification"). Which of these do you enjoy more: playing after finishing homework, feeling that you earned it? Or putting off homework to play, with that sinking feeling that you really ought to be working instead?

Want to Know More?

As part of our training, we've read hundreds of psychology experiments. Most of them are long forgotten, but here's one we really like.

A group of four-year-olds at a Stanford University childcare center were offered a choice. They could have one marshmallow right away, or they could wait 15 minutes and get two marshmallows. Many of the kids ate the first marshmallow almost immediately. Others waited the 15 minutes and got the second marshmallow.

The researchers checked in with those same kids again 14 years later, when they were 18 years old. They found that the kids who'd waited for the second marshmallow could concentrate and handle frustration better. They got along better with other people, too. Plus, the children who had waited for two marshmallows averaged 210 points higher on their college entrance exams than the kids who ate one marshmallow right away.

In short, the kids who waited on marshmallows showed the ability to delay gratification. That ability has big implications for your future life. And it's something you can start practicing now.

Keeping It
REAL

"The hardest thing is actually starting the work. I'll usually avoid starting and play games instead. Then it gets so late that I don't even have time to start."
— *Oliver*

PIGGY BANKING IN REAL LIFE

Here are ways you can delay gratification every day and strengthen Your Mind's Piggy Bank. If you do these things regularly, you'll find it easier to do the same with schoolwork.

Saving

This is the most concrete and direct way to Piggy Bank. Set aside part of the money you get for something larger later. Then watch it grow.

Eating

Everyone gets tempted by foods that aren't so healthy but taste really good. The idea of munching on chips and soda often sounds a lot better than eating veggies and other healthy foods. But sugary and salty foods, while they may taste great now, don't provide many health benefits and can make you feel lousy later. A more healthful diet will lead to feeling better and growing up stronger, with fewer illnesses.

Working

Doing chores or taking on a summer job are excellent ways to practice Piggy Banking. You do real work. You meet the demands of a boss or another adult. And you learn to get along with

coworkers. In return you get a future benefit, such as money or a better job later on.

Waiting

When there's something you really want, hold off a bit. If there's a game you're longing for, ask for it for your birthday and wait. If there's a video you're dying to see, watch it after finishing your chores rather than the other way around.

Practicing

Practice is all about investing effort in something in order to do it better in the future. When you start learning violin, for instance, you're making mainly squeaks and screeches. The benefits come later—slow but steady improvement and truly beautiful music if you stick with it for a long time.

PIGGY BANKING WITH HOMEWORK

Homework is where you need Your Mind's Piggy Bank most of all. Nearly every school night, you find yourself with assignments to do. At the same time, you probably also find all sorts of activities you'd much rather do. How do you choose what you have to do over what you want to do? Even more, how do you choose something that seems boring, difficult, and pointless over something you really love?

You Piggy Bank it, and here's how.

You will need a piggy bank or jar or other container, and a stash of coins. Use any type of coin you like.

STEP 1.
CONSIDER FUTURE YOU

Think about how Present You doing the homework now will help in the future. Make a list that shows how homework will help the Future You . . . tomorrow . . . next week . . . next year . . . in 5 years . . . in 20 years.

STEP 2.
SET YOUR IMMEDIATE GOAL

Write it down and make it specific. Use this sentence model: "I will be good to Future Me by _____." The blank line could say "practicing the bassoon every night" or something similarly specific.

STEP 3.
SET YOUR TIMETABLE

Decide how long you will work toward the immediate goal. It might be one month, one quarter, one semester, or longer. You can also give yourself a reward—a purchase you will make with the collected coins when you've finished.

STEP 4.
MAKE REGULAR DEPOSITS

Every time you complete your immediate goal, such as practicing the bassoon every night, drop a coin into the bank.

STEP 5.
SEE PROGRESS

Watch the coins add up and your benefits grow.

STEP 6.
CASH OUT OR REINVEST

Let's say you decided to invest for a two-month period. At the end of two months, you have a decent size stash of coins in your Piggy Bank—and now it's time to decide what to do with them. You could spend the money on something you want, like the reward you chose in Step 3.

Or, better, you can put it back into the Piggy Bank and build on it. That's called *reinvesting*. Repeat the process of Piggy Banking your homework for another two months. You'll add more money to what you already have and build an even larger stash. And when those two months are up, you can reinvest again. That's Piggy Banking and delaying gratification. The more you can wait, the bigger your reward.

App Demonstration: Louise

After a long, hard, and forgettable day at school, all I want to do in the evening is play World Domination: Epic Clash of Titanic Civilizations. Unfortunately, my mom thinks this is "not a productive use of time." She always nags me to turn it off and do my homework.

Usually I just put her off by asking for five more minutes, and another five, and five more after that. Soon she loses her patience and starts yelling. Sometimes I'll keep playing and put off my homework for hours, or not even do it at all. Then Mom goes totally ballistic.

Eventually, Mom made an appointment with a psychologist, Dr. Whatever, to help us "work on our issues." At first I thought this was really dumb. Still, Dr. Whatever wasn't all that bad. When I found out that he plays World Domination, too, I actually started listening to him.

He explained about working now and getting rewards later, rather than playing now and paying the price later. It sounded good, but really, how can I do that? When it comes down to World Domination versus geography homework, why should I choose geography, even if it's "better for me"?

That's when we came up with my Piggy Bank plan.

STEP 1.
CONSIDER FUTURE ME

I made a list of how doing this homework would help me:

- **Tomorrow:** I'll have it done, and Mom and my teacher won't be disappointed again.

- **Next Week:** This stuff will definitely be on the test.

- **Next Year:** If I get a good grade in geography, I can move up to world history, which I actually find interesting, and it is related to World Domination.

- **In 5 Years:** I really want to study game developing in college, and the competition is intense. Getting good grades will help me get into the program I want.

- **In 20 Years:** When I'm 33, I won't remember anything about this assignment or anything I learned in this class. But I'll still have to do things I don't like doing, so I'd better start practicing now.

STEP 2.
SET MY IMMEDIATE GOAL

I will be good to Future Me by doing homework first and gaming second.

STEP 3.
SET MY TIMETABLE

I decided to work on this for one month. I also decided to save money for new World Domination goods.

STEP 4.
MAKE REGULAR DEPOSITS

I planned to set aside some money from my allowance and my babysitting jobs, and my mom said she would pitch in some extra, too. Each night if I met my Immediate Goal— doing homework before gaming—I would deposit 50 cents in the Piggy Bank.

At first, I didn't stick to the plan so well, and I wasn't earning a lot of coins. It was just too hard to put off something I loved *now* just to get something else *later*. But each time I did earn a coin, it got a little easier the next time. I could see the payoff right there in the bank. Also, once I started doing homework, it didn't feel quite as bad. It was still hard and boring, but I liked the feeling of taking on something hard and boring and getting it done.

STEP 5.
SEE PROGRESS

Within a couple of weeks, Future Me benefits were starting to show up. Teachers liked seeing more homework coming in. My science teacher even called me aside to tell me he'd noticed my "encouraging new attitude." My test grades were creeping up, and Mom and I were fighting a lot less about homework.

Seeing my progress was really motivating, and choosing work before play kept getting more and more doable.

STEP 6.
CASH OUT OR REINVEST

At the end of the month, I'd saved up enough coins to buy new lives and moves in World Domination. But I decided to keep going and build on what I had. I set a new term of three months and a goal of saving enough to buy the second version of the game, Intergalactic Domination. It felt great to get something through my own hard work.

what's your payoff?

Use Your Mind's Piggy Bank	Don't Use It
Work now, play later; study tonight, good grades tomorrow, celebrate on the weekend	Fun now, problems later; play tonight, bad grade tomorrow, grounded on the weekend
Treat schoolwork as an invest-ment in your future	Treat homework as nothing more than an annoyance
Practice a skill, gradually get better at it	Give up the skill because you're not good at it now; never improve

APP 6
YOUR MIND'S
ACTIVATOR

Cease C's and attain A's

Picture this:

You have a test tomorrow morning on George Washington and the American Revolution. To study, you read over your notes and the assigned chapters, and it pretty much makes sense. You get a good night's sleep, chomp down cereal for breakfast, and march confidently into the test. You get a C+.

What went wrong?

Not enough sleep? Unlikely, since you got nine hours. (Useful statistic: Nine hours of sleep is recommended for mental alertness.)

A problem with your choice of breakfast? Very unlikely—while cereal is not the healthiest breakfast you can eat, there's no evidence that it makes any difference in social studies test performance.

Much more likely is that you weren't studying actively enough. You weren't making good use of Your Mind's Activator.

Regrettably, this is a problem for many students. If you just read over your George Washington notes and remember what they say, you're going to get pounded if the test asks something really hard. For the best results, and to shift from C+ to A, you have to actively do something with the information you're studying. That's true for George Washington, geometry, geology—almost any subject at school. This chapter shows you how to shift from passive to active studying.

App Operation

To help you understand the difference between passive and active studying, check out the Activ-O-Meter.

0: Asleep. This is the lowest level of mental activity, and obviously, the worst for studying. Fact: If you study about George Washington while sleeping, you will learn nothing about George Washington. (Though at least you'll feel rested while failing the test.)

1–3: Passive. You're not asleep, but you might as well be. You see and hear information but don't really think about it.

4–6: Recognition. A little better. At this level, you read over the material and understand it. The problem is that "understanding" it is not the same as "remembering" or "explaining" it. Sure, you might understand something when you read it Tuesday night, but that doesn't mean you'll remember it for a test Wednesday morning. It also doesn't mean you'll be able to explain it in an essay or apply it to a new problem.

7–8: Active. Much better. At this level, you're making connections in your mind. And these connections are what enable you to remember and answer best. For example, let's say you learn the definition for the Stamp Act, and even write it down:

> Stamp Act: American colonists had to pay extra taxes for stamped paper.

That's nice, and if the test asks you to define the Stamp Act, you're probably okay. But what if the test asks you to "explain the relationship between the Stamp Act, the French and Indian War, and the American Revolution"? For tests with questions like this (which are common), you need to study more actively. You need to make connections. With the Stamp Act, for example, the important connections are:

1. England had just spent lots of money on the French and Indian War and needed to raise taxes to pay for it.

2. Colonists found this unfair. They started to think about a government of their own.

When you make connections like these, you understand the Stamp Act (or whatever you're studying) in a much deeper way. You're also much better prepared when the teacher asks you difficult questions about it.

9–10: Mega-Active. Best. Here, you do more than make connections in your mind. You extend and apply them to something completely different. This gets into the really intense questions teachers love to dish out, and also the hardest questions on tests. These are questions like, "If you were King of England in 1770, what would you do to stop the revolution in America, and why?" or "How might the Revolution have turned out differently if George Washington hadn't been in command?" When you can answer questions like these, you understand the material a whole lot better.

When you really need to understand something, crank up your mental activity. Here is a four-step method for doing that. Use it when studying for tests.

STEP 1.
PREDICT WHAT YOU'LL NEED TO KNOW

The first step in studying for any test is to know what to study. Sometimes this is very clear: The teacher specifically spells out the topics and questions beforehand. Sometimes, on the other hand, this seems impossible: The teacher doesn't explain or says things that confuse you. Most often, it's somewhere in between: The teacher gives hints and messages, and it's the students' job to figure them out.

Here are some clues:

- **What's been emphasized so far?** If the teacher spent 45 minutes on Battle X and two minutes on Battle Y, expect to see much more of Battle X on the test.

- **What were prior tests like?** "Given that she asked this about Christopher Columbus, and that about the Mayflower, what's she likely to ask about George Washington?"

- **Prepare for the worst.** For example, maybe you're not sure whether the test will ask "Who were the first three presidents of the United States?" or "What was Washington's influence on Thomas Jefferson's presidency?" Don't just cross your fingers and hope for the easy one. Instead, make sure that you can answer both.

Tip. If you're still unsure what will be on the test, ASK the teAcHeR. Many teachers love to help.

"When I have to get ready for tests that have essays, I make a list of possible essay questions. I think of the main things that we covered in class. I predicted one that showed up on the history test we just had!"
—Nicole

STEP 2.
RECALL THE CONTENT

It's usually not enough to be able to recognize the material when you see it. Most tests require that you actively remember it. So when studying, test yourself to make sure you can actually recall what you've studied.

Here's a good method:

- Every time you finish reading a chapter or notes, cover everything below the title for each section. Then retell the content in your own words. This is called *paraphrasing*. If you can do that, make a plus sign (+) in the margin—if not, mark a minus (-).

- Repeat that process until you've earned three plus signs for a section. Now you can be pretty sure you know that material and don't need to review it again until just before the test.

- Move on to other sections until you've earned three plus signs for each section.

STEP 3.
MAKE RELATIONSHIPS

Here's where you crank up into very active thinking. First, think about the *relationships* involved: How is one idea similar to another? How is it different? How did one event lead to the next?

Second, take ideas, which can get pretty abstract, and convert them into visual images—something to actually show the relationships. Three ways to do that are using visual organizers, timelines, and Venn diagrams.

Visual Organizers

These are useful when you have a lot of information. With so much to think about, it's hard to keep it all straight. Visual organizers help arrange the information into one compact space that's easy to see. Check out this example:

⬇ Boston Tea Party ⬇

Causes	Event	Results
_____	When? _____	_____
_____	Where? _____	_____
_____	What happened? _____	_____

⬇ Boston Massacre ⬇

Causes	Event	Results
_____	When? _____	_____
_____	Where? _____	_____
_____	What happened? _____	_____

⬇ Battle of Bunker Hill ⬇

Causes	Event	Results
_____	When? _____	_____
_____	Where? _____	_____
_____	What happened? _____	_____

"What I usually do is I make this big poster with all the things that I need to know, separate it into sections, and look through it all the time. I put it up on my wall and look at it every day."   **—Ruth**

Timelines

These are especially useful for tracking events over time. Timelines can help you see how one thing leads to another and another. Indeed, most major events, like the American Revolution, don't just happen overnight. They build up for a very long time. To keep track of all this and see it clearly, use a timeline. Here's an example:

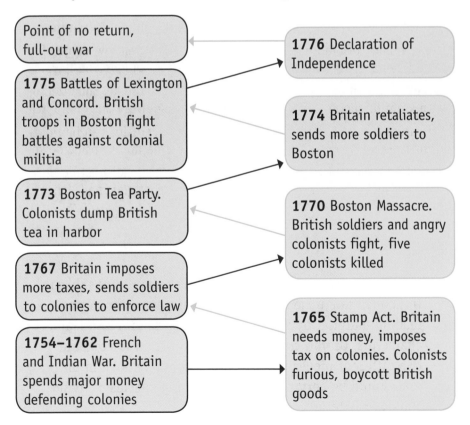

Point of no return, full-out war

1776 Declaration of Independence

1775 Battles of Lexington and Concord. British troops in Boston fight battles against colonial militia

1774 Britain retaliates, sends more soldiers to Boston

1773 Boston Tea Party. Colonists dump British tea in harbor

1770 Boston Massacre. British soldiers and angry colonists fight, five colonists killed

1767 Britain imposes more taxes, sends soldiers to colonies to enforce law

1765 Stamp Act. Britain needs money, imposes tax on colonies. Colonists furious, boycott British goods

1754–1762 French and Indian War. Britain spends major money defending colonies

Venn Diagrams

These are great for the age-old *compare and contrast* questions, such as, "How are George Washington and Ben Franklin *similar and different?*" Even if you don't think questions like that will be on the test, doing Venn diagrams can help you understand the material in a deeper way. To make one, you draw circles to show where the two things overlap (similar) and where they don't (different).

For example, here's a Venn diagram that answers the question "Compare and contrast mustard and ketchup."

Mustard	Both	Ketchup
wide range of brands and flavors	widely used on hamburgers and hot dogs	narrow range of brands and flavors
usually scooped out with knife or spoon	both condiments	usually squeezed or squirted out of a bottle
jars usually right-side up	inexpensive	bottles can be right-side up or upside down
delicious on pastrami sandwich	common at BBQs and picnics	disgusting on pastrami sandwich

Venn diagrams can be useful in just about any subject. In English language arts, you can learn more about your reading material by making a Venn diagram for two major characters. Or you could use a Venn diagram to compare two different pieces of literature. In biology, a Venn diagram could be very useful for comparing species of living things or habitats.

STEP 4.
APPLY AND EXTEND

Apply and extend means you take the material and *apply* it to something new or *extend* it in some novel direction. Many teachers put apply-and-extend questions on tests, and these can be really tough.

There are four types of apply-and-extend questions that pop up again and again. If you can handle these four kinds of questions, you've probably nailed the material. Invent apply-and-extend questions for yourself after you read over your notes or chapters. Then spend time answering them. For extra mind activation, write down your answers.

Here are four typical kinds of apply-and-extend questions:

You Go There

In this question type, you're magically transplanted into a different time and place and asked what you'd do there. This usually takes one of two forms: Imagine that you are somebody famous ("If you were the prime minister of Canada, would you have supported joining World War II? Why or why not?"). Or imagine that you are somebody normal ("If you were a Toronto business owner in 1939, would you support or oppose joining the war, and why?").

This kind of apply-and-extend question works in many subjects. In literature: "Imagine you are the main character in the story. What would you do when you find the lost treasure?" In science: "You've invented a machine that takes you to the center of the earth. What geological layers do you pass along the way, and what dangers do you face at each layer?"

They Come Here

This is the flip side of the "You Go There" question type. In this format, someone famous is transported to the here-and-now and you're asked to explain his or her position on some modern-day issue. For example, "If Darwin were alive today, what would he think about global climate change?" Or "If a *T. rex* reappeared on Earth, on what continent would it best flourish?"

What-If

In these apply-and-extend questions, you consider what would have happened if important events had turned out differently. For example, "If England had defeated the American Revolution, how would your life be different?" What-ifs can also be used for literature by asking questions like "How would the story be different if the main character had not answered the doorbell?" Or in science: "What if a meteor landed in the Pacific Ocean—how might our lives be affected?"

Evaluate

In this apply-and-extend format, you're given a statement and asked to agree or disagree and explain why. For instance: "Evaluate the statement 'Power companies should create much more electricity from wind.'" In this case, your job is to evaluate both sides of the argument—reasons why power companies should use more wind and reasons why they shouldn't. Then choose one side or the other and support it.

Robert

App demonstration: Robert

Math is my hardest subject at school. I used to dread math tests. But last semester I started using my mind's Activator to prepare for tests, and I have been doing a lot better. Here's how I'm preparing for my next test.

STEP 1.
PREDICT WHAT I'LL NEED TO KNOW

For the past two weeks, we've been going through Chapter 6 about analyzing data. My teacher, Ms. Z, has also spent forever talking about mean, median, and mode. We measure mean, median, and mode in all kinds of ways: temperatures for particular time periods, population growth over time, popularity of different YouTube videos. As a result, I'm almost positive that she'll put something like that on our test.

Also, when I think back to the last couple of tests, I noticed that she starts out with easy problems like in the homework. Then the last few are always "stretch questions." I bet she does the same for this test.

STEP 2.
RECALL THE CONTENT

To make sure I can recall mean, median, and mode from memory, I cover up the definitions I wrote in my notebook. Then I retell them in my own words. I also make up examples of each. Once I can do that correctly three different times, I know that I've got it.

* Mean is the mathematical average. The mean of 8, 9, and 19 is 12 (8 + 9 + 19 = 36, and 36 divided by 3 equals 12).

* Median is the <u>middle</u> number. The median of 8, 9, and 12 is 9.

* Mode is the most common or "popular" number (what's in fashion or in mode). The mode of 8, 9, 12, 12, 17 and 19 is 12.

STEP 3.
MAKE RELATIONSHIPS

Unfortunately, just being able to state the definitions won't get me all that far on the test. Knowing Ms. Z, I'll probably also have to compare and contrast all three: how are mean, median, and mode similar and different from each other? Time for a Venn diagram:

Mean

☆The average figured out by adding all the numbers in the group together and dividing by the total numbers in the list

Mean & Median

☆May not be a member of the list of numbers

M, M, & M

☆Reseachers use M, M, & M when analizing data

☆The M, M, & M are numbers that represent the list of numbers

☆M, M, & M are different kinds of averages

Median

☆The number in the middle when the numbers are listed in order

☆When there are 2 middle numbers, the median is the mean of those 2 numbers

Mode

☆The number that appears in the list of numbers most often

☆If no one number is listed more than the others, there is no mode

STEP 4.
APPLY AND EXTEND

To get ready for Ms. Z's stretch questions, I apply and extend.

First, I come up with different situations or sets of data. Second, I ask which one works best for each—mean, median, or mode—and why. (This is totally the kind of thing Ms. Z loves to put on tests.) Third, I answer the questions.

Which Work Best? Mean, Median, or Mode?

1. Given the following test scores, how did the class do on last year's math final? 83, 87, 88, 95, 92, 89, 99, 86, 52, 55, 60

2. How many students come to school by foot, bus, train, car, or bicycle?

3. What's the average of the following yearly salaries among professional hockey players? $2 million, $1.5 million, $2.5 million, $2 million, $2.25 million, $1.75 million

Answers

1. Median is the best measurement here. Because there are outliers (52, 55, 60), those scores pull the mean way down, making the class average look too low if using a mean. (The median is 89.)

2. Mode is best here. Mode means "what's the most common value," and this question is asking about the most common form of transportation.

3. Trick question. Mean, median, and mode all come out to $2 million here.

APP PRACTICE

Here is a reading about a topic from history. This kind of reading can be boring and hard to focus on. Imagine you now are going to face a test on this topic. Use Your Mind's Activator to learn it well and prepare for the test.

Asian Nobility of the 18th Century

In Asia during the 18th century, nobles were the highest class of society. Nobles were only one step below the ruler. Although they enjoyed wealth, power, and prestige, they were tightly controlled by their rulers. In Japan, that ruler was the shogun. In China, it was the emperor.

Japanese nobility were called *daimyo*. Daimyo were military lords who had power over a large territory given to them by the shogun. The shogun controlled the daimyo by forcing them to spend every other year in the capital city of Edo. During years when daimyo went back home to their estates, their family members were required to stay in Edo. The shogun figured that daimyo would be less likely to attack him if their family members were living nearby. The shogun also kept the daimyos' wealth in check by forcing them to contribute money to help build roads, bridges, and urban buildings.

In China, the political power and influence of nobles was diminished by a merit testing system. Many top-ranking government officials were required to pass a difficult academic test rather than simply inheriting their jobs. There was also a complicated ranking system that prevented families from keeping too much power. Very often, a noble's oldest son could only inherit a rank one step lower than his father's. Earlier in history, Chinese nobility were forced to live in Beijing. They could only leave if given permission by the emperor.

Follow the four steps of Your Mind's Activator.

1. PREDICT WHAT YOU'LL NEED TO KNOW

The first step in preparing for this imaginary test is to figure out what will probably be on it. Start by predicting questions for the test, and be sure you can answer them. When doing this, consider the following:

- What are the most important points in this reading? (And therefore what is the teacher most likely to ask?)

- What issues in this reading has the teacher emphasized the most in class?

- What kind of questions has the teacher asked on prior tests?

Better yet, put yourself in the teacher's shoes and make up the test yourself. What are the best questions to ask about this reading? When you imagine you're teaching, that's very active. You're selecting what's important and explaining it in a way that makes sense.

2. RECALL THE CONTENT

Test yourself to be sure you can actually recall what you've read. Do the +/- review. Go back to the reading and check off whether you can paraphrase each section from memory. When you earn three + marks on Japan, move on to China.

3. MAKE RELATIONSHIPS

Think about how Japanese and Chinese nobility were similar and how they were different. Make a Venn diagram: two overlapping circles that visually show the similarities and differences.

4. APPLY AND EXTEND

To get your mind Mega-Active, answer the following questions:

1. If you were a noble in the 18th century, would you rather live in Japan or China? Why?

2. If the Japanese daimyo took over the U.S. Congress tomorrow, would it work better, worse, or no differently? Why?

what's your payoff?

Use Your Mind's Activator	Don't Use It
Earn better grades	Earn poorer grades
Connect and get engaged with schoolwork	Sit back and stay bored
Go deep, answer hard questions	Stay on the surface, answer easy questions
Make connections that register information in your mind	Forget stuff right after you learn it

APP 7

your mind's workbench

Just what was I supposed to do next?

Your Mind's Workbench is a place in mind for holding information while working on it. This is also called "Working Memory." You use it for remembering one thing while thinking about something else.

You need Your Mind's Workbench for just about everything in school. For example, think about what actually happens when your teacher says, "Take out your math book, open to page 39, and do exercises 1 through 18." The first thing you do is look for your math book. But while you're looking for the book, you hold the page number and exercise numbers on Your Mind's Workbench.

Here's another example: When you multiply 42 by 6 in your head, you might first compute 40 x 6. Then you'd hold that product (240) on your Workbench while you multiply 2 by 6 and add that product (12) to the 240 to reach your answer: 252.

Sounds easy, but here's the catch: Your Mind's Workbench has a very small amount of space, and big problems arise when space runs out. When something new comes into your mind, it can push other information right off.

App Operation

Workbench space is precious. With so little available, you've got to make the best use of it. To do that, use the following two strategies: "Keep off what can stay off," and "Use your workbench better."

KEEP OFF WHAT CAN STAY OFF

Anything you don't load onto Your Mind's Workbench is one fewer thing your Workbench has to hold on to. To help keep your Workbench clear, use the following four simple ideas:

1. Write stuff down

Once you've recorded information somewhere, you no longer need to hold it on your Workbench. To test this, compare doing 47 x 23 on paper to doing 47 x 23 in your head and see which turns out better.

Say you have half a dozen things to do: empty the dishwasher, water plants, email your teacher, practice the tambourine, fold laundry, and take out the garbage. Write them out as a list so you don't forget about the garbage while focusing on the dishwasher and plants.

Paper is great for lists—as long as you don't lose the paper. If you use a smartphone or other electronic device and look at it often, it might make a lot of sense for you to create your lists on it. Just be sure not to lose your device!

2. Use cell phone reminders

If there's something you constantly forget to do, set your cell phone (or other device) to alert you when it's time to do it. You can also have your phone give you reminders at different times.

> *"A lot of times I put things in my phone, so it reminds me at a certain period during the day. Then I upload it on Google Calendar as well, so I can plan for the future. I use my phone so much, it makes more sense to use it rather than paper notes because I always have my phone with me. It reminds me when I need to be reminded."*
> **—Mitch**

Keeping It **REAL**

3. Set up routines

Get tasks on automatic pilot. When you can do things routinely and automatically, you don't have to stop and think about them. This frees up space on your Workbench for things you really *do* have to think about. For example, if you always keep your school planner in the same place, you don't have to use up precious memory space trying to remember where you left it. If you always practice the tambourine for 15 minutes right after dinner, you don't have to figure out how to fit it into your schedule.

4. Reduce outside interference

For most kids, the major issue here is listening to music. If you're listening to current hits on your headphones while reading about ancient civilizations in your textbook, the music will compete with the history for Workbench space. That makes it harder to remember your reading.

If you just can't tolerate silence while studying (many people really cannot), listen to instrumental music. Since it has no words, it doesn't clutter your Workbench as much as music with lyrics. Ongoing background sounds such as a fan or running water (like a stream or fountain) also work for some people.

WAYS TO USE YOUR WORKBENCH BETTER

Even with all the Keep Off What Can Stay Off strategies, there will still be plenty of times you just can't keep information off your Workbench. For those times, you need to use your Workbench better. Here are five tactics.

1. Make meaning

Your Mind's Workbench has very limited space. However, your long-term memory is almost limitless. Long-term memory is where you store things that you know and understand.

So, when there's too much information (TMI) for your mental Workbench, plug it into your long-term memory, which has all the space you'll ever need. For example, a group of vocabulary words from a science chapter is hard to remember as a list: observe, lab, reactions, chemical, microscope, heat, experiment. Definitely TMI. But if you can give those words some kind of meaning, you can plug them into your long-term memory. You can do that by creating a meaningful sentence: "In my lab experiment, I observe heat and chemical reactions under a microscope." The sentence makes sense, and memorizing it allows you to move it to long-term memory. That makes it easier to remember.

2. Combine and conquer

Normal human beings can only hold four or five items of information on their mental Workbench at any time. To remember more than that, you can combine smaller items into bigger ones—and conquer what you need to remember.

Try it out. First, try to remember these numbers: 3, 0, 8, 6, 2, 9, 4, 8, 7, 5. For most people, this is too much to keep on their Workbenches. Instead, combine and conquer that list by dividing it into three easy chunks, like a phone number: 308-629-4875.

You can combine and conquer letters, too. Read the following letters and try to remember them: M, V, C, O, B, T, N, C, S, B, N, H.

Remembering that string is almost impossible, because it's 12 items of information. That's more than almost anyone can hold on his or her mental Workbench. So instead, combine those 12 items into groups: MTV, HBO, CNN, CBS. This is so much easier to remember because now there are only four units to remember. And those units have meaning, too.

3. Make an image

When you put something on your Workbench in picture form instead of in words, you save lots of space. For instance, compare the verbal explanation of Newton's second and third laws with a visual depiction. Which is easier to remember?

Verbal: Newton's second law states that how quickly an object changes movement depends on how hard it is pushed or pulled and its mass (how much material is in the object). Newton's third law says that when one object applies a force on a second object, that second object applies an equal and opposite force on the first object.

Visual: Most people find the visual explanation much easier to remember. Obviously, when a giant truck hits a tiny bug, the bug changes its movement and splats.

Similarly, when a giant bug hits a smaller truck, the truck changes its movement and splats.

Also, if you read Chapter 3, you'll remember the CAFE approach to making pictures. In case you skipped that chapter (or forgot it), CAFE is a way of making pictures really come to life. First, there's plenty of COLOR. Second, the pictures include ACTION. Third, the images have FEELING—emotions and extra senses (sound, smell, taste). Fourth, there's EXAGGERATION: tiny bugs and giant trucks, or giant bugs and tiny trucks, which is not your normal collision.

4. Use mnemonics

A *mnemonic* is a trick for remembering things. One of the most common ones is to make a sentence using the first letters of items on your list. This is a great way to combine information and create meaning.

For example, take the *Hierarchy of Classification* for all living beings: Kingdom, Phylum, Class, Order, Family, Genus, and Species. Remembering all this is neither easy nor fun. Much easier, and not entirely un-fun, is to create a mnemonic. For example, "King Phillip Came Over For Good Spaghetti." Alternatively, there is "Kind Patriots Can Order Fried Goose Samples." And "Kentucky Predators Create Oddly Flavored Gorilla Stalkers." Or "Keep Putting Chocolate On Five Greasy Sandwiches."

Invent a sentence that makes at least some logical sense, and it will be fairly easy to remember. To translate that sentence back into the seven levels of classification, you use the first letter of each word in the sentence as a reminder of the first letter of the word you need to remember.

5. Use pegging

If you're having trouble remembering multiple pieces of information, then connect them to things you can remember. That's called "pegging in memory."

For instance, many people find the phyla in the kingdom Animalia very difficult to recall. At the same time, most people find major body parts very easy to remember. So, to better remember the things you can't remember, like phyla in the kingdom Animalia, "peg" them to things you can, like body parts.

Consider the following seven major phyla in the kingdom Animalia: sponge, jellyfish, worm, squid, insects, sea stars, mammals. To learn these, you can mentally peg each one to a body part. To help make the pegs more memorable, use CAFE: Color, Action, Feeling, and Exaggeration.

Item	Peg	Visualize Them Together
Sponge	Top of head	A coral sponge is being squished on top of my head. I feel the saltwater in my eyes, taste it on my lips, and smell it as it drips down my nose.
Jellyfish	Face	A giant glow-in-the-dark jellyfish has attached itself to my face.
Worm	Arms	A thousand slimy green worms slither down my arms.
Squid	Belly	The squid's tentacles have wrapped around my belly, and their suction cups are super-tight.
Insects	Hips	Dragonflies, butterflies, and moths are all attached to my hips, with their wings fluttering furiously to lift me up in the air.
Sea stars	Legs	Rainbow-colored sea stars are wrestling for space on the fronts of my legs.
Mammals	Toes	I'm a mammal, and last night I stubbed my big toe in the dark.

These images are kind of fun and should be easy to remember. Next time you need to recall these phyla, like during a test, you can simply recall the images you created to go with body parts. Start at the top—with your head—and you'll remember the idea of a sponge on top of it. Continue down your body, and those images will come to mind—and with them, the phyla.

Besides body parts, you can also peg things to the rooms in a house or anything else that's easy to remember.

App Demonstration: Fiona

I guess you could say I am a busy kid. I'm in track and field, which is a big commitment. And I'm taking mostly advanced classes at school, so I have a lot of homework. I

Fiona

can also get pretty scattered—my friends call me "Flaky Fiona." It's a good thing I learned how to use my mind's Workbench. Here's a typical day in my life.

MORNING

After I get up, I have to shower, get dressed, stretch out my sore hamstrings from track practice, clean the kitchen, pack my gym clothes, and feed the fish. While I'm doing all this, the gym clothes can easily fall off my Workbench. I've already shown up empty-handed at PE three times this month!

So I found a way to take the gym clothes off my Workbench. I write myself a simple note the night before: "Gym clothes!" I slap it on the bathroom mirror and immediately see it when I brush my teeth the next morning.

This way, my gym clothes become one less thing to hold on my Workbench—or to fall off it.

OUT THE DOOR

Unfortunately, getting out the door is not nearly as simple as saying good-bye and walking away. I wish. I have many things to gather together and take along: keys, glasses, lunch money, planner, homework, and books. I often used to forget about one while racing around the house looking for another. To solve this, I now keep all of the smaller items together in a bowl on top of my dresser. I also pack up my books and homework the night before and leave them next to the bowl. This way, I can easily and quickly locate them every morning—leaving much less to remember and much less on my Workbench. (Did anyone say "less stress"?)

SCIENCE CLASS

We're learning the stages of mitosis: how cells divide and reproduce. Not surprisingly, these stages are pretty tough to remember—interphase, metaphase, anaphase, telophase, and cytokinesis. To make it easier, I created a mnemonic from the first letter of each stage: "I Made A Terrible Cake."

MATH CLASS

To free up my mental Workbench in math, I make it a point to do as much work as possible on paper and as little as possible in my head. We're learning how to divide fractions, and I'm still not totally clear on the steps to follow. So instead of trying to hold all the steps on my Workbench—and forgetting one while working on another—I drew up a diagram that spells out each step.

To Divide Fractions

$$\frac{a}{b} \div \frac{c}{d}$$

Step 1: Turn the second fraction upside-down.

$$\frac{a}{b} \div \frac{d}{c}$$

Step 2: Change the sign to a multiplication sign.

$$\frac{a}{b} \times \frac{d}{c}$$

Step 3: Multiply the top numbers with each other and the bottom numbers with each other.

$$\frac{a \times d}{b \times c}$$

LUNCH

My new friend Carla invited me to her house for lunch. Here are the directions Carla gave me:

"Walk out the school's west door. Go 300 yards and take your second right onto 12th Street, then go 200 yards and take your third left onto 2nd Street. After passing Howling Harry's Hardware Store on your left, turn right at 4th Street, and go to the sixth house on the left. If you reach 1st Avenue, you've gone too far."

Clearly, this was way too much to remember. I pretty much lost track of what she was saying somewhere around "Walk out the school's west door." It's okay, though. I didn't even try to remember. I just entered her address into a mapping site and got the directions there. The info never even touched my mental Workbench.

LANGUAGE ARTS CLASS

Our assignment: "Compare and contrast the use of fore-shadowing in *Tom Sawyer* and *Anne of Green Gables*."

To save my Workbench, I wrote an outline of my answer. Rather than trying to remember what to write as I was writing, I referred back to the outline as I went along. I also wrote two separate drafts. In the first, I focused exclusively on my ideas. In the second, I cleaned up spelling, punctuation, and grammar. That way I wasn't trying to remember all those rules while still trying to hold ideas about Tom and Anne on my Workbench.

HEALTH CLASS—LAST PERIOD

To remember my speech in health class about the six basic nutrients, I mentally pegged each nutrient onto one of my body parts and then visualized an action to go with it.

Nutrient	Body Peg	Visualized Action
Carbohydrates: Beans, fruit, grains	Toes	I kick a bean-shaped watermelon into a goal filled with wheat and rice.
Protein: Eggs, cheese, milk, meat, and tofu	Knee	I balance a big plate of scrambled eggs and tofu on my knee.
Fat: Nuts, oils, avocados	Belly	I slather oil on my stomach.
Minerals: Calcium, iron	Hands	My hands are as strong as iron.
Vitamins: A, B, C, D, E	Mouth	I shout out the letters of the alphabet with my mouth wide open.
Water	Face	I stick my face into a rushing waterfall on a beautiful tropical island and feel the cool liquid pouring down.

App Practice

Do these exercises to practice the strategies for managing Your Mind's Workbench.

MNEMONIC

Create a mnemonic to help you remember the five largest cities in Finland:

- Helsinki
- Espoo
- Tampere
- Vantaa
- Turku

FIXED PLACE

In your home, decide on a fixed place for the items you need to take to school every day. Put these items in this place every evening. Here's a list of common things that students take to school. Use the list as a starter, and add to it (or subtract from it) so that it works for you.

- Textbooks
- Notebooks and folders
- Planner or calendar
- Laptop or tablet
- Backpack
- Cell phone
- Keys
- What else?

PEGGING

Imagine you have to bring the following seven things home from school today. How will you remember them all? Peg each one to a body part and visualize an action or CAFE image to go with it.

Item	Body Peg	Visualized Action
Geometry homework	Feet	The red laces on my shoes criss-cross to make geometric shapes
Greek myths book		
Habitats research		
Gymnastics gear		
Attention Apps lunchbox		
Permission slip for class trip to the ballet		
Spelling test from last Friday		

what's your payoff?

Here are examples of what can happen when you use Your Mind's Workbench—and what can happen when it gets overloaded.

	Workbench Working	Overloaded Workbench
Reading	You remember what you read at the top and middle of a page, then tie that together with what you read at the bottom	By the time you reach the bottom of the page, you forget what you read at the top and middle; you only remember the last thing you read
Writing	You remember *what* you want to write about while also remembering grammar, punctuation, and spelling	You forget about spelling, grammar, and punctuation while you focus on writing down thoughts
Math	You remember all the steps of an equation or problem while working on each step	You lose track of what to do next
Directions	You remember *what* to do while thinking about *how* to do it You remember directions while working on a task	You forget the question while looking for an answer You forget what you're supposed to be doing in the middle of doing it
Ideas	You hold an idea in your mind while working and developing it	You forget the second idea while discussing the first one When comparing and contrasting two things, you lose track of your ideas about one while thinking about the other

App 8

Your mind's speedometer

Going 80 down the highway and 8 down the alley (not vice versa)

School is a marathon, not a 100-yard dash. To run it and win it, you have to pace yourself and go at the right speed. The App for controlling speed is Your Mind's Speedometer. It lets you match your speed to the road conditions—or in this case to the school conditions.

When work is easy and clear, you speed up and zoom straight ahead. When the going gets tricky and curvy, you go more slowly. In other words, with easy problems you can race right through. But with harder problems, you need to slow down and proceed with caution.

If you don't use Your Mind's Speedometer well, you may end up working too quickly or too slowly. Either can lead to a MAJOR MALFUNCTION.

MAJOR MALFUNCTION: ACCIDENTS

By far the most common problem is *speeding*—working too quickly. If we drive down a narrow side street at 70 mph (the same speed we drive down an interstate highway), we'll probably get in an accident or get a speeding ticket.

It's the same thing with schoolwork. If you try to do $3697 \div 261.3$ at the same speed as $36 \div 2$, you'll probably make careless errors—mistakes you wouldn't have made if you were working at the right speed.

MAJOR MALFUNCTION: PERFECTIONISM

A slightly less common but still nasty speed problem is perfectionism—working super-slowly in order to avoid mistakes and get everything right. If we drive down the highway at 15 mph (the same speed we drive down a narrow side street), it will take forever to get where we're going.

This idea applies to work you do in school, too. If you work through a whole test of simple math facts at the same speed you use for long division with decimals, you probably won't make careless errors. But you'll be lucky to finish half the test.

App Operation

To operate Your Mind's Speedometer, you match your speed to the task at hand. Here are the speeds.

- **Slow/Crawling.** At this speed, you're working very carefully and deliberately.

- **Medium/Cruising.** You're cruising along and working at a steady pace.

- **Fast/Racing.** Full speed ahead: You barely have to worry about accuracy and mistakes because the work is so easy.

Follow these guidelines to choose the right speed and make sure you *stay* at the right speed.

FIND THE RIGHT SPEED

To find the right speed, look at the work you have to do and answer the following four questions.

Question #1: How hard is this for me?

Basically, you go more slowly at things that are hard for you and faster at things you're good at.

Use Slow/Crawling for:

- Work that's really complex and requires multiple steps, like long division

- Work that's really hard to understand, like Shakespeare
- Work that's new—you just learned it and don't get it yet

Use Medium/Cruising for:

- Work you sort of get, but still need to think through or check your notes on
- Work you've studied and already know, but might need to review
- Work that's new or strange within a subject you generally pick up quickly—like renal anatomy, even if you're good at science

Use Fast/Racing for:

- Work you've done many times already
- Work you can do almost without thinking about it
- Work you could almost do in your sleep

Question #2: How much time will it take (and how do I know that)?

Okay, that's actually two questions. But they go closely together. When deciding how long a task will take, consider *how* you know that. Generally, you know by comparing how long a similar task took before. If a long-division worksheet took half an hour last week when you were still learning the material, it will probably take less time this week when you know it better. If tonight's science homework is much harder than last night's, it will almost definitely take more time.

Question #3: How much time do I have?

Say you're taking a math test, and you have 20 minutes left for three long-division items. You have the luxury of slowing down and doing them very carefully. If you have only 5 minutes left and you still have eight items to do, you'd better speed up.

The same applies to homework. If you're working on a mythology project that's due tomorrow morning, you have to go at a higher speed than if it's due next week. Worse, if it's midnight and the project is only half-finished, you'll need to crank up into Racing just to get it done.

Question #4: What else needs to get done?

Say you're working on an astronomy project that's due next week. But you also have projects due next week in health and English language arts. That means you'll have to work on the astronomy project at a higher speed than if you were just doing astronomy alone.

> Keeping It REAL
>
> *"My tip is, don't try to be a perfectionist. If you get that bogged down in one assignment, thinking that it has to be just perfect, then you won't have time for everything else. You have to give time to everything. I'm still learning to do that!"*
>
> —Hailey

BE YOUR OWN TRAFFIC COP

Monitor your speed to ensure that you're not going too fast or too slow. Here are four ways to do that:

1. **Use time landmarks.** Compare where you should be to where you are when working on assignments and tests. If you see that you're halfway through a test halfway through the test period, you're probably working at the right speed. But if you're only one-third done and the period is half over, you ought to speed up a little. If you're one-tenth done, you'll have to *really* speed up.

2. **Use a timer.** When studying, use your phone, clock, watch, or other timer. If possible, set it to alert you at certain "speed checkpoints." For a one-hour study session, tell it to buzz you at 20 and 40 minutes. Then you can check to make sure you're working at the right pace. Be sure to build in the checkpoints at key intervals—early enough to make changes. If you check your speed 50 minutes into a 60-minute assignment, it may be too late to speed up.

3. **Know how long things really take you.** If it usually takes you five minutes to read a page in your history textbook, give yourself half an hour to read a six-page chapter.

4. **Get help.** If all else fails, have an adult check in with you periodically to help monitor speed.

TIPS FOR THE HABITUAL SPEEDSTER

Lots of people love the thrill of fast driving, and lots of students love working fast, too. It feels like you "win" if you finish first—though of course you don't really win anything at all. In fact, you're much more likely to lose as a result of speeding and making careless mistakes.

If you're a speed demon, here's a good way to turn things around: Remove the payoff for finishing fast.

For example, let's say you're going out to play basketball, which you love, as soon as you finish biology homework, which you don't love. You've created a major incentive to speed. Instead, build in a set period of study time, study for that whole period, then reward yourself afterward.

If you tell yourself, "I can practice basketball as soon as I finish bio," you'll want to do bio at Racing speed.

Instead, tell yourself, "I'll work from 6 to 7 and practice after that." This gives you less reason to finish in 15 minutes at Racing speed, since you'll still have 45 minutes of work left anyway. Also, if you finish the assignment in under an hour, you can use the remaining time for better quality: Go back and check your work, study the concepts again, or prepare for an upcoming test.

Lots of people also race through work they're not good at because they want to get it over with. Doing that only makes the problem worse. If you're having trouble with an assignment, slow down and work it out. Think it through, work deliberately, check your notes, look for answers online, or ask a teacher or friend for help.

"If I go through the test super-fast, I lose lots of points. It doesn't work for me when teachers let us out early when we finish the test, especially in the class right before lunch. So I have to tell myself that if I rush through the test and get done early, the teacher and my parents won't be so impressed with the grade, and neither will I." —Marcus

App Demonstration: Ann

I actually don't mind school that much. I'm good at most of my subjects, with the very large exception of math, which is deadly. My problem is working at the right speed. I think I can whip through everything at Racing speed. But, well, that doesn't always work out so well. Now that I'm learning how to manage my mind's Speedometer, things are going a little better.

Ann

Here's how I'm tackling my schoolwork this week.

Task	Write two paragraphs in French about my spring break.
How hard is it for me?	Not at all. I love French and have a good vocabulary, so I usually don't need to look up many words.
How much time will it take (and how do I know that)?	About one hour. Last month I wrote a paragraph in French about the seasons in 30 minutes; two paragraphs should take about twice as long.
How much time do I have? What else needs to get done?	I have less than one hour Monday night. It is the only assignment that's due Tuesday, but I need to save some time to spend on math and science.
Select a speed	Racing ➜

Be my own traffic cop 	Check that I'm about halfway done after 20 minutes, and nearly done at 40 minutes.

Task	Complete items 1–30 on pages 111 and 112 of the math workbook: dividing fractions and decimals.
How hard is it for me?	Very. I have been really lost in this unit; I bombed the last test.
How much time will it take (and how do I know that)?	Over two hours. Math homework usually takes at least an hour, even when I know what I'm doing, and this is a lot of problems.
How much time do I have? What else needs to get done?	It's due in two days, so I have two nights. French is due tomorrow, but then I can focus on math.
Select a speed	Crawling
Be my own traffic cop 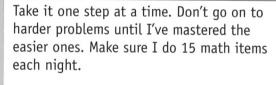	Take it one step at a time. Don't go on to harder problems until I've mastered the easier ones. Make sure I do 15 math items each night.

Task	Write a book report on *The Ranger's Apprentice*.
How hard is it for me?	Not too hard. I love the book so far, but I'm not quite done. Book reports seem kind of dumb to me, but I can do them.

How much time will it take (and how do I know that)?	Five hours. The last book report I wrote took about three hours, but I need to add in time to finish the book!
How much time do I have? What else needs to get done?	I have all week, since this isn't due until next Monday.
Select a speed	Cruising
Be my own traffic cop 	I will spend two hours on Wednesday, one hour each on Thursday and Friday, and one hour over the weekend. I plan to finish the book Wednesday and do the writing over the next few days. If I'm not done with the book on Wednesday then I know I'm off the pace and need to work faster.

Task	Finish reading *The Survival Guide for School Success*.
How hard is it for me?	It's so not hard. I get everything in every chapter—best book I ever read.
How much time will it take (and how do I know that)?	I average 5 minutes per page on schoolwork if I'm focused. But I love this stuff, so I can read even faster.
How much time do I have? What else needs to get done?	I don't have much time at all! All the Attention Apps are urgently needed now.
Select a speed	Racing
Be my own traffic cop	Make sure I don't get so carried away with this that I ignore other work.

App Practice

To practice using Your Mind's Speedometer, photocopy the worksheet on page 119, download it or make your own version. Write a task you have to do in the top space, such as a homework assignment, test or quiz, even a chore at home. Then fill out the rest of the spaces using the App Demonstration on pages 114–117 as a model. Start new worksheets for all your challenging tasks.

What's Your Payoff?

Use Your Mind's Speedometer	Don't Use It
Work at the right speed to do a good job	Work too quickly and make careless errors or work too slowly and never get done
Adjust speeds; match your speed to the conditions	Get stuck in one speed; work at the same pace, regardless of what's really needed
Avoid careless errors; show what you really know	Make careless errors; lose points needlessly

YOUR MIND'S SPEEDOMETER

Task	
How hard is it for me?	
How much time will it take (and how do I know that)?	
How much time do I have? What else needs to get done?	
Select a speed	
Be my own traffic cop	

App 9

Your mind's Calendar

Linking what to do with when to do it, without double-booking

Spider-Man has a lot going on. In addition to being a superhero, he's a physics student at Columbia University, a photographer for the *Daily Bugle,* and a regular guy. Mary Jane, whom he's loved since the comic book first started, is engaged to somebody else. Aunt May, who raised him, is in danger of being evicted from her home.

Let's look at Spider-Man's schedule for today:

8:00 a.m.	*Daily Bugle* staff meeting
9:00 a.m.	Fight Doctor Octopus, save New York City from uncontrolled killer tentacles
10:45 a.m.	Pick up laundry
11:00 a.m.	Midterm exam on rotational energy
12:30 p.m.	Stop bank robbery, grab some lunch

1:30 p.m.	Photo shoot at mayor's press conference, City Hall
2:15 p.m.	Physics lecture on Gauss's law for gravity
3:30 p.m.	Text Mary Jane "I love you," order flowers for her
3:45 p.m.	Battle more super-criminals: dehydrate Hydro-Man, suck up Sandman with vacuum cleaner
5:30 p.m.	Coffee and doughnut break
5:45 p.m.	Physics discussion group on Faraday's law of induction
7:00 p.m.	Meet with Aunt May's attorney, file court papers, eat dinner
8:00 p.m.	Death struggle with Green Goblin: Save tramway car full of kids dropped from bridge, save Mary Jane dropped at same time, avoid being impaled by remote control glider, impale Green Goblin instead
10:30 p.m.	Pick up souvlaki sandwich on the way home
11:00 p.m.	Relax, watch *Batman* reruns
11:45 p.m.	Lights out

What would happen if Spider-Man didn't manage his time well? At the very least, New York City would be overrun by weird super-criminals.

If you don't manage your time well at school, the consequences are only slightly less scary: running late and scrambling to finish work, last-minute rush jobs, constant time pressure and stress.

What you need is Your Mind's Calendar.

App Operation

Before you start using Your Mind's Calendar, check out these three tricky qualities about time. We call them time buts.

1. **Time is everywhere, but you can't see it (or hear it, taste it, etc.).** That means it's hard to track time

without the proper tools. These include calendars, clocks, and timers.

2. **Time is infinite, but yours isn't.** *Your* time is limited to 24 hours a day. Actually, when you subtract the time you spend on basic activities like sleeping, eating, and sitting in school, you have very little time left to do the things you want to do—and the things you *have* to do.

3. **Being in the moment in time is great, but not at school.** You know that feeling when you're doing something you really love? It's as if time doesn't matter. All that matters is what you're doing right then and there. But how often do you feel like that about schoolwork? At school, *all* time matters—it's not just what's happening at that moment. It's what's due tomorrow and next week, and how Monday's assignment affects Friday's quiz.

Your Mind's Calendar helps you get a better handle on time buts. It's a tool for prioritizing, managing, and executing everything you need to do—with less stress. To use it, follow these steps.

STEP 1.
GET A CALENDAR

A calendar visually shows the relationship between minutes, hours, days, and weeks. So it's a really useful way to *see* your responsibilities along with how much time you have to do them.

Pick a calendar that works for you. They come in two basic types: physical and electronic. Make sure your calendar shows the hours of the day. Also make sure you can record information next to those hours. You might get a physical (paper) version from your school. Electronic calendars for your phone, tablet, or computer include iHomework, Google Calendar, and others.

Make sure you find a calendar you like, because you need to *use* it for it to do you any good. More on that coming up.

STEP 2.
MAKE A TO-DO LIST

This should include everything you have to do; not just schoolwork. Put down chores, sports, clubs, music practice, time with friends, and anything else you need to do.

STEP 3.
PRIORITIZE YOUR TO-DO LIST

Remember: Your time is limited. You simply don't have enough time to do everything, and if you try to, it's trouble. You end up juggling too many things at once, starting things you can't finish, and getting frustrated. To avoid this, you need to *prioritize*—to decide what's more and less important.

To help with this, use this Importance Meter to organize your to-dos. Put each thing you need to do into one of the importance categories.

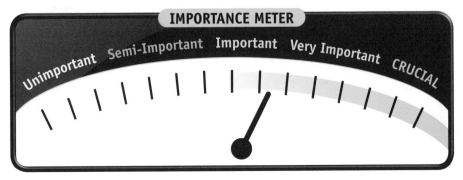

- **Unimportant.** Put things in this category if you don't need to do them or if it doesn't matter when you do them. These are things that can easily wait until later.

- **Semi-Important.** Put things in this category that you ought to do but can do later if necessary.

- **Important.** These are things you should do now.

- **Very Important.** These are things you *have to* do now.

- **Crucial.** Save this category for those things that you absolutely, positively *must* do now—or else suffer big consequences.

Projects "Due" vs. "Do"

If a project is *due* on October 9, that doesn't mean you *do* it on October 8. For projects, you really need to use Your Mind's Calendar. Spell out a plan showing what parts you'll do two weeks ahead, one week ahead, three and two nights ahead, and on the last night.

STEP 4.
FILL IN YOUR CALENDAR

Start by writing down things that you always do or that are part of regular life. These are things like sleeping, eating, and school. Add those to the hours when you do them, like in this example:

	Monday	Tuesday	Wednesday
6:00	Sleep		
6:30			
7:00	↓		
7:30	Shower & get dressed		
8:00	Breakfast and pack		
8:30	for school		
9:00	School		
9:30	↓		

→

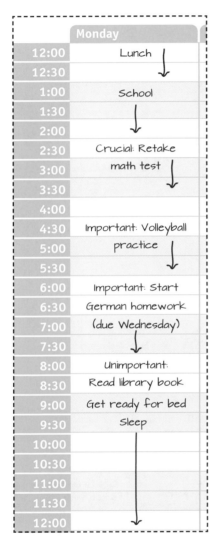

	Monday
12:00	Lunch
12:30	
1:00	School
1:30	
2:00	
2:30	Crucial: Retake
3:00	math test
3:30	
4:00	
4:30	Important: Volleyball
5:00	practice
5:30	
6:00	Important: Start
6:30	German homework
7:00	(due Wednesday)
7:30	
8:00	Unimportant:
8:30	Read library book
9:00	Get ready for bed
9:30	Sleep
10:00	
10:30	
11:00	
11:30	
12:00	

Next, add the items from your to-do list, starting with anything you listed as "Crucial." Crucial items need to appear on today's date as early as you can do them. Next, fill in items you listed as "Very Important," fitting them into today's date if at all possible. As you move down your list, adding things that are less important, they can go further out on the schedule (to later days).

As you're adding your tasks to your calendar, be realistic about how much time each one will take and when you'll be able to do it. Think about the past and the future. First, look behind you: How much time did this task (or a similar one) take in the past? When you did it before, did you have enough time? Too much? Too little?

Next, look ahead. Even though you may have lots of time available today, tomorrow and the next day may be very different. Do your best to match each task to the right time slot. See a sample calendar on pages 126–127.

	Sunday	Monday	Tuesday
6:00		Sleep	Sleep
6:30		↓	↓
7:00			
7:30		Shower & get dressed	Shower & get dressed
8:00		Breakfast and	Breakfast and
8:30		pack for school	pack for school
9:00		School	School
9:30			
10:00			
10:30			
11:00			
11:30		↓	↓
12:00		Lunch ↓	Lunch ↓
12:30			
1:00		School	School
1:30			
2:00		↓	
2:30		Crucial: Retake	
3:00		math test ↓	
3:30		↓	↓
4:00			
4:30		Important:	
5:00		Volleyball practice	
5:30		↓	
6:00		Important: Start	Very Important: Call Grandma
6:30		German homework	(it's her birthday!)
7:00		(due Wednesday)	Important: Finish
7:30		↓	German homework
8:00		Unimportant:	Unimportant:
8:30		Read library book	Read library book
9:00		Get ready for bed	Get ready for bed
9:30		Sleep	Sleep
10:00			
10:30			
11:00			
11:30			
12:00		↓	↓

Wednesday	Thursday	Friday	Saturday	
Sleep	Sleep	Sleep		6:00
				6:30
↓	↓	↓		7:00
Shower & get dressed	Shower & get dressed	Shower & get dressed		7:30
Breakfast and pack for school	Breakfast and pack for school	Breakfast and pack for school		8:00
				8:30
School	School	School		9:00
				9:30
				10:00
				10:30
				11:00
↓	↓	↓		11:30
Lunch ↓	Lunch ↓	Lunch ↓		12:00
↓	↓	↓		12:30
School	School	School		1:00
				1:30
				2:00
				2:30
↓	↓	↓		3:00
		Very Important: Yearbook meeting		3:30
				4:00
Important: Volleyball practice		↓		4:30
				5:00
↓				5:30
				6:00
				6:30
				7:00
				7:30
	Semi-Important: Watch favorite TV show	Crucial: Go to Sandy's party		8:00
				8:30
Get ready for bed	Semi-Important: Chat online about the TV show	↓		9:00
Sleep				9:30
				10:00
↓	Get ready for bed	↓		10:30
	Sleep	Get ready for bed		11:00
		Sleep ↓		11:30
↓	↓	↓		12:00

The best calendar system in the world has zero value if forgotten and neglected in the bottom of a backpack or book bag. You need to check it regularly to remind you what you have to do. We recommend checking it at these three important times every day:

• In the morning before you go to school, to preview your day.

• After school, to keep you on task for homework and other after-school activities.

• Before bed, to make sure you did everything you had to that day, and to preview the next day.

You will also want to check your calendar anytime something new or unexpected comes up during the day. If a buddy calls you to come over and play zombie tag with kids in his neighborhood, you need to make sure there isn't anything else you should be doing during that time instead.

Keeping It REAL

"I customized the ringtone on my phone so that I don't have to think about it. When I hear that ringtone, I'm like, 'Oh, I have to do homework.'"

—Marcus

STEP 6.
DO YOUR WORK

Now all that's left is doing the work you put down in the time slots. If you wrote that you'd study for your Spanish test from 8:00 to 9:00, that's what you should be doing then.

app demonstration: Fabio

I have always had trouble managing time. I always think things will be fine and I'll get them done no problem. But then my deadlines sneak up on me! Here's how I started using my mind's Calendar to do better with that.

Fabio

STEP 1.
GET A CALENDAR

I've tried paper calendars, but somehow I always lose them. I found an online calendar that works much better for me. It's harder to lose, and I can take it with me almost everywhere I go.

STEP 2.
MAKE A TO-DO LIST

On Sunday night, I wrote up my to-do list to get ready for the week. Here it is: health project, make posters for the school carnival, science homework, make appointment to get haircut, get ice cream with Vanessa, trombone lessons, swim team practice.

STEP 3.
PRIORITIZE MY TO-DO LIST

- Science homework is Crucial. It's due Tuesday. If I don't turn it in I'll get a zero, and my grade will go down to a D.

- Ice cream with Vanessa is Very Important. If I blow her off again, she'll get really upset.

- My health project is Important. The final paper is due next week, so I need to have all the research done by the end of this week.

- Trombone lessons are Important. If I don't go to trombone, my dad gets really mad about the money he's spending on lessons. Plus, I kind of like it.

- Swim team practice is Important. If I miss, Coach makes me swim extra laps at the next practice.

- Carnival posters are Semi-Important. I told the carnival director I'd get them done soon, but she'll understand if I take a bit longer.

- Haircut appointment is Unimportant. My hair looks great as it is.

STEP 4.
FILL IN MY CALENDAR

Sunday	Monday	Tuesday	
	Sleep	Sleep	6:00
	↓	↓	6:30
			7:00
	Shower & get dressed	Shower & get dressed	7:30
	Breakfast and	Breakfast and	8:00
	pack for school	pack for school	8:30
	School	School	9:00
			9:30
			10:00
			10:30
			11:00
			11:30
	Lunch	Lunch	12:00
	↓	↓	12:30
	School	School	1:00
			1:30
			2:00
			2:30
	↓	↓	3:00
			3:30
		Important:	4:00
		Trombone	4:30
		lesson	5:00
		↓	5:30
			6:00
			6:30
Crucial: Science	Crucial: Finish	Important:	7:00
homework	science homework	Research	7:30
↓	↓	health project	8:00
			8:30
	Get ready for bed	Get ready for bed	9:00
	Sleep	Sleep	9:30
			10:00
			10:30
			11:00
			11:30
	↓	↓	12:00

	Wednesday	Thursday	Friday	Saturday
6:00	Sleep	Sleep	Sleep	Sleep
6:30	↓	↓	↓	
7:00	↓	↓	↓	
7:30	Shower, get dressed	Shower, get dressed	Shower, get dressed	
8:00	Breakfast and	Breakfast and	Breakfast and	
8:30	pack for school	pack for school	pack for school	↓
9:00	School	School	School	Shower, get dressed
9:30				
10:00				Important:
10:30				Swim team
11:00				practice
11:30	↓	↓	↓	
12:00	Lunch ↓	Lunch ↓	Lunch ↓	Lunch ↓
12:30				
1:00	School	School	School	
1:30				
2:00				Unimportant:
2:30				Haircut
3:00	↓	↓	↓	
3:30				
4:00	Very Important:	Important:		
4:30	Ice cream	Trombone lesson		
5:00	with Vanessa	↓		
5:30	Important:			
6:00	Swim team	Semi-Important:		
6:30	practice	Posters for		
7:00	Important:	school carnival		
7:30	Research health	Important:		
8:00	project	Research health		
8:30		project		
9:00	Get ready for bed	Get ready for bed	Get ready for bed	
9:30	Sleep	Sleep	Sleep	
10:00				
10:30				Get ready for bed
11:00				Sleep
11:30				
12:00	↓	↓	↓	↓

STEP 5.
CHECK MY CALENDAR AT REGULAR TIMES

I check my calendar at least three times each school day. First, I check it in the morning to look ahead at my day. Second, I check it after school to see what's going on then. Third, before going to bed, I check it to make sure I've done everything and preview the day ahead.

Also, when something excellent and exciting comes up, I check to see if I actually have time for it. Like last Wednesday after school, my friend Ming invited me over to watch *The Simpsons*. This sounded great. I'm really into *The Simpsons* (and even more into Ming). But my calendar for Wednesday was crammed. So we scheduled for another date.

STEP 6.
DO MY WORK

Okay, putting "Science Homework" on the calendar doesn't *make* me do the homework. But it does help. First, when I know that time is all set on my calendar, I stress less. That makes homework easier to deal with. Also, once it's on the calendar, I don't have to waste time at night figuring out when to do it. By this point, I've learned that it works to follow the calendar: If the calendar says do it, I do it.

app practice

Follow these steps to start using Your Mind's Calendar.

STEP 1.
GET A CALENDAR

See page 122 for guidelines on how to choose one.

STEP 2.
MAKE A TO-DO LIST

While you're first getting used to using a calendar, just list things you need to do over the next one or two days. Include schoolwork and non-school responsibilities. As you get more comfortable with your calendar, you'll want to work a week and even several weeks in advance. You can always add or subtract things on your calendar after you fill out a week.

STEP 3.
PRIORITIZE YOUR TO-DO LIST

You can use the Importance Meter on page 123. Or you can make your own categories of importance.

STEP 4.
FILL IN YOUR CALENDAR

Remember to include your automatic tasks, like sleeping and eating, as well as everything on your to-do list. Refer to past time frames to help figure out how much time to allow for your tasks. Think to the future to help decide when to do things.

STEP 5.
CHECK YOUR CALENDAR AT REGULAR TIMES

Figure out when you'll check your calendar, then practice doing it every time. Keep the calendar someplace where you'll remember it. Your backpack is a good place for the school day. But you might keep it on your desk or by your bed when you're not at school.

STEP 6.
DO YOUR WORK

Now, do the work during the times you have set to do it. Keep track of time so you don't get surprised when time passes more quickly than you thought. Test yourself, too: Partway through an activity, estimate how much time you have left on the clock. Then actually check the clock to see how close you are. If your estimates are usually on-target, that means you're accurately sensing the passage of time.

After you practice this process for a couple days, you're ready to start using Your Mind's Calendar full time.

what's your payoff?

Use Your Mind's Calendar	Don't Use It
Complete the tasks that need to be completed	Spend too much time on unimportant tasks while forgetting something really important
Keep a clear sense of how much time is passing and how much you have left	Lose track of time
Get things done early and on time	Constantly be late and rushed
Stay on top of time	Get crushed by time

APP 10

YOUR MIND'S OBSERVER

How not to act clueless

Meet Clueless Guy. He's nice enough, and he means well, but he's clueless. What makes him clueless is that he's lost his mind's Observer. His Observer is what gives him the ability to watch himself in a situation, check how he's doing, and change what he's doing if it's not turning out well. (How he lost his mind's Observer remains a mystery.)

Without his mind's Observer, Clueless Guy is unaware how others see him. In the cafeteria, he tells a joke and laughs as if it's the funniest thing ever. He doesn't notice that nobody else is laughing. In the hallway, he sees class-mates talking and barges right in. He doesn't notice that he's totally unwelcome.

And then there's Clueless Gal. The poor girl has classroom problems. After finishing work, Clueless Gal

hands it in right away, repeatedly making mistakes she would have found if she'd just stopped to check it over. On tests, she often overestimates how well she did, then gets let down by the actual result. Her report cards also have a nasty habit of coming out far worse than she expected.

Most likely you're not *that* clueless, but Your Mind's Observer still can help you. You use it to watch how you're doing and make changes when you're not doing so well. It helps with schoolwork and social life.

Want to Know More?

The psychology term for this skill is *self-monitoring*. According to *The American Heritage Dictionary*, a monitor is "one that admonishes, cautions, or reminds, and particularly with respect to matters of conduct." In plain English, a monitor is someone who watches you to see that you're doing the right thing and reports you or takes action when you're not. Monitors commonly include hall monitors, bus monitors, cafeteria monitors, and so on.

Self-monitoring is doing that with yourself—observing your own behavior, reporting to yourself if it's not turning out well, and taking action to fix it.

app operation

Your Mind's Observer is a tool for—you got it—observing yourself. There are three Key Functions to Your Mind's Observer.

"Reading" Other People

People often mean lots of things above and beyond what they actually say. Listen for *tone of voice,* or how they say it. For instance, saying "Great!" in an excited voice has almost the opposite meaning of saying "Great" in a sarcastic way. Also, watch body language. People often show what they're thinking and feeling by their movements and facial expressions, not just by their words.

KEY FUNCTION 1: WATCH PEOPLE'S REACTIONS

Notice how other people react to what you say and do. If you're telling a friend about your visit to the ostrich farm over the weekend, and he starts yawning or looking away, use Your Mind's Observer to see that he's losing interest.

KEY FUNCTION 2: LEARN FROM MISTAKES

Messing up, which everyone does every day, can provide very valuable information. By using Your Mind's Observer, you can look at your mess-ups and see what you did wrong. Even better, seeing what you did wrong also tells you what to fix and what to do differently next time.

KEY FUNCTION 3: USE THE PAST TO GUIDE YOU

The best predictor of how things will turn out in the future is how they turned out in the past. If you told a joke yesterday that everyone found dopey or offensive, don't retell it today in the hope that it will go over better. Instead, open Your Mind's Observer, look back to yesterday's result, and consider that while deciding what to say and do now.

> **Keeping It REAL**
>
> *"If I say three things and the person I'm talking to hasn't said anything, I know I better ask that person a question instead of keep talking."* —Yuki

Besides social situations, these three functions also apply to just about every aspect of schoolwork. With Your Mind's Observer, you can watch what you're doing to make sure you're doing it right. For example:

Homework
Before starting, preview the directions. Make sure you know what you're supposed to do before doing it. While working, watch yourself. Make sure you're doing what the directions actually say. When finished, review and revise. Find mistakes and fix them.

Writing
Review your papers before turning them in.

- The simplest way is to reread them yourself. This can be annoying, sure. But if you've already gone to the trouble of writing a paper, one last read-through isn't too much.

- Another way is to have someone else read your paper to you so you can hear how it sounds. If asking someone to read your papers aloud seems strange to you, the computer you're using might have speech capacity or text-to speech software. Programs such as NaturalReader (www.naturalreaders.com), many of which are free, will read aloud what you've written and let you correct what doesn't sound right.

Tests

- Read instructions carefully.

- Proofread short answers and essays before turning in the test.

- On bubble answer sheets, watch yourself to make sure that your answers are entered on the right answer line. (Using the wrong line can be hazardous to your grade.)

- When you get your test back, don't just look at your grade. Look at what you did right and wrong. In particular, check your errors. Identify *why* you made them and what you'll do to avoid repeating them on the next test.

- Evaluate your studying. Did you study the right material? Did you study actively enough? (See App 6.) Did you start studying early enough?

Keeping It REAL

"I highlight the verbs in test questions. That forces me to think about what I'm supposed to do and what the question is really asking me." **—Nicole**

In Class

- When working in groups, listen to others' ideas, even if you're sure yours are better. When others disagree with you, consider their opinions, even if you think you're right.

- Observe other students. Look at what the A students are doing in class. Compare that to what other students are doing. Adjust what you're doing to match the kids who get the best grades, as much as possible.

App Demonstration: Clifford and Kari

We're two good friends, but opposites in many ways. Check out this table to see what we mean.

Clued-In Clifford	**Clueless Kari**
Considering Other People's Reactions	
I told a fart joke during book club the other day, and nobody laughed. I even noticed a couple of the other kids make a scrunched-up face, like "Ew." I will never tell that kind of joke at book club again.	My friend Lana won't sit by me at lunch anymore. I heard from a friend that she doesn't like my excessive burping. She never *said* she didn't like it, though. How was I supposed to know?
Responding to Mistakes	
In gym we've been practicing running the mile. The first time, I got really tired by the end and couldn't finish. I realized that I'd started too fast and didn't save enough energy for the finish. Next time, I paced myself better.	I also got wiped out by the end of the mile, but I didn't think about it much. Next time we ran the mile, I ran out of energy at the end again. I guess I'm just no good at running. ➜

Clued-In Clifford	Clueless Kari
Benefiting from the Past	
Before studying for my next history test, I'm thinking about how I studied for the last one. I didn't do as well as I'd hoped. I remember that I felt pretty panicked as I tried to study the whole chapter in one night. This time I'm giving myself three nights.	Oh, boy. I didn't do too well on the last history test, either. And I am *not* excited about taking the next one. I don't even want to think about that test until I absolutely have to. It's just my style to put things off.

app practice

Take the quiz on pages 143–144 to help you understand Your Mind's Observer. You can make a photocopy of the page and write your answers on there, download it, or write your answers on a blank sheet. For your Occasionally Clueless and Seriously Clueless answers, make a plan to change.

what's your payoff?

Use Your Mind's Observer	Don't Use It
Learn from experience and use that to change	Ignore prior experience; don't change, repeat mistakes
Realistically judge your own strengths and weaknesses	Believe you're great at things you're not so good at; think you did much better than you really did
Adjust what you're doing based on other people's responses	Be unaware of others' responses; keep on doing what you're doing regardless of results
Pick up on clues and use them	Be clueless

how clueless AM I?

From *The Survival Guide for School Success* by Ron Shumsky, Susan M. Islascox, and Rob Bell, copyright © 2014. Free Spirit Publishing Inc, Minneapolis, MN; 800-735-7323; www.freespirit.com. This page may be reproduced for individual, classroom, and small group work only. For other uses, go to www.freespirit.com/company/permissions.cfm.

ARE YOU SERIOUSLY CLUELESS?
CHECK A BOX UNDER EACH SCENARIO BELOW.

I do this often = *Never Clueless*

I do this sometimes = *Occasionally Clueless*

I do this seldom = *Seriously Clueless*

Learn from mistakes

☐ Often/Never Clueless   ☐ Sometimes/Occasionally Clueless   ☐ Seldom/Seriously Clueless

If Occasionally or Seriously Clueless, what will I do differently this week?

_____

_____

Respectfully exchange ideas in groups; contribute to discussions without dominating or quitting

☐ Often/Never Clueless   ☐ Sometimes/Occasionally Clueless   ☐ Seldom/Seriously Clueless

If Occasionally or Seriously Clueless, what will I do differently this week?

_____

_____

When finished with a test, check over answers before handing it in

☐ Often/Never Clueless   ☐ Sometimes/Occasionally Clueless   ☐ Seldom/Seriously Clueless

If Occasionally or Seriously Clueless, what will I do differently this week?

_____

_____

how clueless Am I? (continued)

Review errors on a test to see why I made them and what to do differently next time

☐ Often/Never
Clueless

☐ Sometimes/Occasionally
Clueless

☐ Seldom/Seriously
Clueless

If Occasionally or Seriously Clueless, what will I do differently this week?

_____

_____

Read over papers before turning them in

☐ Often/Never
Clueless

☐ Sometimes/Occasionally
Clueless

☐ Seldom/Seriously
Clueless

If Occasionally or Seriously Clueless, what will I do differently this week?

_____

_____

Pay attention to other people's reactions—tone of voice, facial expressions, body language

☐ Often/Never
Clueless

☐ Sometimes/Occasionally
Clueless

☐ Seldom/Seriously
Clueless

If Occasionally or Seriously Clueless, what will I do differently this week?

_____

_____

Before giving feedback to others, consider how they'll react

☐ Often/Never
Clueless

☐ Sometimes/Occasionally
Clueless

☐ Seldom/Seriously
Clueless

If Occasionally or Seriously Clueless, what will I do differently this week?

_____

_____

they're your
apps—use them

All the Attention Apps help you control attention, but
each in its own way.

Consider a toolbox containing a hammer, screwdriver,
pliers, saw, and six other tools. They're all involved in con-
struction, but each one does something different. What's
important is to match the right tool to the right purpose.
If you use a hammer to cut wood and a saw to bang nails,
you'll get lousy results in carpentry.

The same idea applies to your Attention Apps. To
ensure that your Apps really work, it's important to use
the right one at the right time. To help you remember which to use when, we've created the chart on the
next page.

	What It Does	Use It When . . .
Site Selector	Controls what to think about	. . . your mind wants to go off somewhere else but you need it to stay on the task at hand
Pizza Cutter	Cuts work down to size	. . . work seems like too much or too overwhelming to take on
Video Screen	Shows the benefits of working	. . . work seems pointless
Cheerleader	Encourages you to keep trying and keep going	. . . you're giving up and knocking yourself down
Piggy Bank	Helps you delay gratification so you get less benefit now but more later	. . . choosing between something you really want to do and something you really have to do
Activator	Sets your mind to the right activity level and controls how actively to think	. . . you have to gear up your mind, especially when studying for hard tests
Workbench	Provides a place to store things in your mind while working with them	. . . following multiple steps or instructions . . . remembering what you just read or heard while reading or listening to something new

→

	What It Does	Use It When . . .
Speedometer	Controls how fast you work and helps you balance speed and accuracy	. . . you're working so quickly that you make careless errors or so carefully that you never finish
Calendar	Helps you manage your time	. . . you think you can do eight things at once (even though you can't) . . . you have lots to do and need to plan it out
Observer	Enables you to watch yourself and see how you're doing	. . . you're missing your own mistakes and not learning from what you did wrong

Lifelong benefits: top 8 tips

In addition to using your Apps at the right time, it's important to use them for a *long* time. These Apps aren't just clever little gadgets; they're lifelong skills and habits. Here is a countdown of our top eight tips for using your Attention Apps long-term.

8 **Perform regular tune-ups and adjustments.** If you've been motivating hard work by picturing summer vacation, you'll need a new picture in September. If you're psyching up with the *Rocky* theme song, it's eventually going to lose its punch and need a replacement. In other words, to keep your Apps working, it's important to update them and install new versions.

7 **Create your own Apps.** The 10 Apps in this book are by no means a complete list. What else does your mind do to control attention? Notice this and add it to keep your Apps fresh and meaningful.

6 **Pick and choose.** Let's say you perform an attention function very well. Take speed controls, for example. Perhaps you work quickly enough to get things done, and carefully enough to be accurate. This doesn't mean you don't need Your Mind's Speedometer. Instead, it means you're already applying it well. In this case, it still helps to be aware of the Speedometer App so that you understand what you're doing right to control speed. Beyond that, however, put more practice into Apps you need to work on.

5 **Use them with somebody else.** Show friends, parents, or teachers what you're doing. Get their opinions on how well the Apps are working and how you can use them better.

4 **Use your Apps often.** As with just about every skill, the more you use an App, the better you'll get—and the better it will work. It may take time to master. Avoid trying an App once or twice, concluding that it doesn't do much, then junking it. To get the real benefit, you may need to keep trying.

3 **Combine Apps.** You don't build a house with just a hammer or a screwdriver—you need many tools. Mentally, too, there are many tasks for which one App is not enough. Writing long essays, for example, requires Your Mind's Site Selector for staying on task, Your Mind's Pizza Cutter for slicing into sections, Your Mind's Cheerleader for working hard, and Your Mind's Activator for gearing up. So if you find one App isn't getting the job done, bring in reinforcements.

2 **Treat your Apps with the value they deserve.** Your Attention Apps may not cost any money, but they still have lots of value. If you use them regularly, you'll get more out of them than the most expensive smartphone app ever.

1 **Attention is your mind at its best.** When you're focused, motivated, and organized, you're totally on top of school. Your Apps are fully loaded and ready to go. Use them!

acknowledgments

Here is our short list of the many people who've helped us out. To all those inadvertently omitted or forgotten, *moshiwake gozaimasen*.

Max Bell provided much of the inspiration for this project from the very beginning.

Also, huge thanks to the students at ASIJ who are the kids who provided quotes for this book. Your names are changed, but you know who you are: Ali, Daphne, Hailey, Kenta, Marcus, Mimi, Mitch, Nicole, Oliver, Ruth, Thomas, Vlad, and Yuki.

Sincere gratitude to Karen Noll ("Comma-sama"), Kathy Krauth, Brigid Flannery, and David Islascox, who reviewed our many drafts, continually providing help and encouragement. Nancy Kroonenberg also reviewed early drafts thoroughly and insightfully. Min-Jin Lee provided further writing advice from someone who writes a million times better than we do.

More special thanks to Eddie and Rebecca and the whole Phillips clan for their excellent ideas and inimitable spirit; Mark Kline, who inspired Dr. Whatever in Chapter 5; Ben Kline for reading and critiquing, Alina Shumsky for reading—and approving!—and Gail Hochman for her prescient insights into the publishing process.

Very different thanks to Abe and Adaia Shumsky, for showing what is good and Mah Tov. Also to Bob and Helen Ann Cox for being such great role models.

And certainly, further thanks are due to our editor Eric Braun, who devoted massive effort to shaping this book and making it what it is.

index

meet the authors

Ron Shumsky, Psy.D., is a clinical psychologist and child neuropsychologist. He specializes in turning abstract psychology concepts into practical language and easy-to-use tools to help kids and teens do better in school. Ron studied and worked in the United States, and now lives in Tokyo with his wife, two kids, and a little dog named Pickles.

Susan M. Islascox, M.A., is a learning support teacher at the American School in Japan who loves the adventure of helping high school students get focused, organized, and motivated. Her students have proven to be her best teachers, and their lessons inform just about everything in this book. Susan lives in Tokyo with her husband and son.

Rob Bell, M.Ed., spent much of his school career doodling in the back row. As an adult he moved to the front of the class and became an elementary school teacher. Rob's imagery and imagination help make it possible to "see" attention in this book—not just read about it. He currently lives and works in Santiago, Chile, with his wife and fellow teacher Christina, son Max, and daughter Maya.